Unburdened

SHEDDING THE FEAR OF MAN
AND WALKING LIGHT AS A CHILD OF GOD

In memory of my dad, Alvis R. Forbes, a man who feared the Lord

And with prayers for the hearts of my five children:

Elisa Joy,

Sadie Pearl,

Raina Abigail,

Hope Julianna,

and our precious new baby, whose arrival should coincide with the release of this book!

May you always walk light in God's grace, and serve Him with joyful abandon.

You are the poem He is writing to the world!

CONTENTS

CHAPTER ONE:
Who Do We Fear?

The year is 1986. I sit at a short wooden desk, my skinny six-year-old legs crossed at the ankle as I bend studiously over the paper in front of me. I select a red crayon from the yellow box and begin to gently etch soft, neat lines. I am pleased with the way the colors look on the page and I smile as I draw the final curve of my rainbow. Setting the crayon in the groove of my desktop, I glance around at the other students.

Curly red hair tumbles over the face of the girl next to me. She is chewing her lip as she draws, and when her right hand reaches up to push the wayward shock of hair out of her eyes, I see her picture. Her butterfly picture is nice, but it's not as good as mine, and that makes me happy.

The two boys in front of me are just scribbling, doodling wavy lines that intersect without order.

I scan the next row, and my eyes rest on the flowered dress and blunt pixie-cut of the new girl. Ana. She joined our class a week ago. On Monday, Mrs. McCann handed her a blue reader—the same color as mine—and sent her down the hall with me to read aloud with the second-graders. Yesterday, she bookmarked Ana's math text near the end, telling her to skip ahead to Lesson 124. The same lesson I am working on.

As one of the older students in my kindergarten class, and an early, avid reader, I find school easy. And because school comes easily, I have earned the admiration of my pretty, brown-eyed teacher. She likes me. She thinks I am smart.

At least I think she does.

Something tightens in my chest as my gaze lingers on Ana's desk. Her picture is beautiful. The colors are bright, vivid. She has drawn a bird, a tropical bird, and somehow the dimensions are right and the wings seem ready to flap right off the white sketch paper.

I tear my focus away for a moment, but my attention snaps back when I see Mrs. McCann approach Ana. "What a beautiful picture. You have so much talent, Ana, and I can tell you worked really hard on your bird. It's just lovely! Amazing, really." Ana beams.

The bell trills. Recess. There is a shuffling of papers and stomping of feet as fifteen kindergartners shrug on coats to head outside to the playground. I dawdle, watching my classmates file happily out of the room.

As I close my crayon box, I watch Mrs. McCann wave the teacher from next door into the classroom. "Come see this," she says, her voice filled with awe. The other teacher walks briskly to her side. I listen to the trip-trap of her heels and hope they don't notice I am still at my desk. "Our new girl, Ana, is a brilliant artist. See this? Look at the colors." The other teacher murmurs her appreciation of Ana's masterpiece. "I had to move her up a level in reading and math, too. She is so far ahead of my other students. And such a sweet girl."

The tightness in my chest swells. I can barely breathe. I want her to like me. I want her to think I am special! The approval of my teacher matters to me more than anything, and I am afraid I have lost it. I tried. But I am not good enough!

Desperately I pull the crayons back out. I add bold strokes to my light lines, trying to make my colors match the vibrant hues of Ana's picture.

Suddenly Mrs. McCann is at my side. "Honey, you've drawn a nice rainbow. Put it away for now and head out to recess with the others." I look up and nod my head. Stuffing the rainbow picture into the back of my desk cubby, I swallow tears.

Six years later, my older sister and I sign up for a week of church camp that includes a two-day backpacking adventure. I know that at end of the week the counselors will give an award for the "Camper of the Week." I covet that award, and I am determined to be perfect so they will choose me.

I smile big as I lace up stiff boots and I sing silly songs to encourage my friends when they get worn-out on the steep hills. I memorize all the Bible verses and sit attentively during the teaching times. I don't complain, and I help two squabbling girls settle a disagreement. I don't talk after lights out, and I get up as soon as the morning alarm sounds. I am friendly and kind and thoughtful. I help wherever I can.

On a day hike, I stumble and fall in an icy alpine creek. I am soaked through and shivering for the rest of the day, with no extra clothes. One of the counselors takes pity on me and I find myself hiking in a pair of wool pants sized for a full-grown man. I laugh at myself, thank the counselor, and try to be brave.

I do all the right things, but I do them for the wrong reasons. My kindness is not spilling over from a heart in love with Jesus. I *do* love Him. As a young girl, Jesus had saved me through the gospel caricatured on a flannel board and stale graham crackers eaten with apple juice in a Sunday school room filled with squirming preschoolers. A faithful teacher had held my hands and prayed with me, and I grasped the truth that I was a sinner and Jesus was my rescuer. Childlike, I hold tight to His love, and I love Him back as much I know how. But the truth is, I can't see Jesus the way I can see people. Jesus doesn't offer me the tangible affirmation my young heart seeks. I love Jesus; I just love the approval of people more. Here at camp, I want to be thought well of. I want to be approved of. I want them to notice my goodness.

And they do. At the ceremony on the last night of camp, the director presents me with a certificate. "Camper of the Week."

I am thrilled. I did all the right things, and they saw. They approved. And for the moment, I feel I am enough in their eyes.

Over-achiever. People-pleaser. Perfectionist. Goody two shoes. Codependent.

There are many names for people like me. People who have spent their lives trying to earn the approval of those around them. People who have hid pride and fear behind a mask of external righteousness. Trying desperately to be good so others might notice their goodness.

As a little girl, I often woke up in the middle of the night to brush my teeth and remake my bed before sliding back under the covers. I couldn't bear the thought of a rumpled bed or dirty teeth, even under the cover of blackest night.

I was a skinny, awkward bookworm with bony knees and thick glasses. I wasn't naturally outgoing or bubbly; I was quiet, timid, and nervous socially. I was clumsy and uncoordinated when it came to schoolyard games. I was never going to be the prettiest, or the most popular, or the team captain. I knew that. So, I set out to be smart. To be good. To earn the approval of others through flawless math tests and perfect behavior.

I was controlled by the fear of what other people were thinking when they saw me. I constantly looked around me for approval, instead of looking to Christ and resting in His grace. Consequently, I lived my life with an inward focus, preoccupied with self rather than focusing outward on glorifying God and loving His people.

Maybe you can identify with this. Maybe you, too, have spent your life lugging around a heavy and awkward burden you were never meant to carry.

Can you picture this? We are walking the bumpy, rock-strewn path of our earthly lives. Christ has rescued us from our sin, set us free from slavery. "So if the Son sets you free, you will be free indeed!" the Bible says in John 8:36 (ESV). He has equipped us with everything we need to walk the path He has prepared for us. 2 Peter 1:3 says, "His divine power granted to us all things that pertain to life and godliness, through the knowledge of him who called us to his own glory and excellence."

But we turn to begin our journeys, and instead of looking upward at Christ, we reach down and we grab hold of a large lumpy knapsack. Instead of cherishing the freedom of our redemption and renewal in Christ, instead of looking to Him alone to meet our needs, we cling to this strange load. We carry with us the weight of our desire to please others, to conform to others' expectations, to be perfect apart from the record bestowed on us by Christ.

It's a heavy burden to carry, and it weighs us down on our journey.

The Bible calls it fearing man. Proverbs 29:25 says, "The fear of man lays a snare, but whoever trusts in the Lord is safe."

Contrasted with the fear of man is the fear of God. Psalm 112:1 tells us, "Praise the Lord! Blessed is the man who fears the Lord, who greatly delights in his commandments!"

We are meant to fear God. Fearing man entangles us.

In a later chapter, I will talk about the gift of salvation, and about the justification and sanctification the Lord so graciously applies to our messy, muddled lives when He saves us. For now, I want to focus on the journey we begin after our salvation is assured. I want to delve into those two options we have in responding to the new life we've been given. We can continue seeking worldly glory and being preoccupied with the opinions and thoughts of the people around us, or we can drop that lumpy weight and walk in the freedom and wisdom of fearing God alone.

So, what's the difference? And why does it matter?

The Israelites were commanded to fear God. Over and over, God revealed His nature through mighty acts on their behalf. He parted seas, He rained down manna, He toppled fortresses and knocked over entire enemy armies. The Israelites had seen God's glory. And He commanded their reverence. He asked His people, the people He had set His affections upon and chosen as His beloved, to worship Him alone.

"And the Lord commanded us to do all these statutes, to fear the Lord our God, for our good always" (Deuteronomy 6:24).

What did that mean for the Israelites? We hear the word "fear" and we think of a small child cowering under a Minnie Mouse comforter, shaking as she imagines the monster lurking beneath her mattress. Obviously, trembling anxiety is a part of the definition of fear, but just as clearly, it's not the whole definition. God was not commanding His beloved people to simply cower before Him, terrified by His power to destroy them. Or was He? He certainly had that power.

According to the *International Standard Bible Encyclopedia*, fear is "a natural and, in its purpose, beneficent feeling, arising in the presence or anticipation of danger, and moving to its avoidance; it is also awakened in the presence of superiors and of striking manifestations of power, etc., taking the form of awe or reverence."[1]

Let's unpack this a little, because I think the fear of the Lord commanded in Scripture actually does encompass both parts of the definition. It's a struggle to wrap our heads around the whole concept, but the creator God is worthy of both our trembling and our awe. James 2:19 tells us "You believe that God is one; you do well. Even the demons believe—and shudder."

Even the demons—beings who stand in opposition to Jesus Christ—fear God and tremble before Him.

When the Israelites were moving through the Promised Land, conquering every nation that had a hold inside its bounds, they were striking the fear of the Lord into the people of the region. When they came to Jericho, Rahab told the spies, "For we have heard how the Lord dried up the water of the Red Sea before you when you came out of Egypt and what you did to the two kings of the Amorites who were beyond the Jordan, to Sihon and Og, whom you devoted to destruction. And as soon as we heard it, our hearts melted, and there was no spirit left in any man because of you, for the Lord your God, he is God in the heavens above and on the earth beneath" (Joshua 2:10-11).

Doesn't it sound like God's enemies were hiding under the covers? They so feared His destruction that their spirits were melted. Later, Gideon led an army of three-hundred men to defeat the Midianites. They raised torches and sounded trumpets, and the enemy army fled in fear before the power of God. God's enemies were right to be afraid of God.

"'To whom then will you compare me, that I should be like him?' says the Holy One" (Isaiah 40: 25). Our God is beyond compare and He is worthy of fear. When God's glory passed over Moses as he was hidden in the cleft of the rock, Moses returned with his face glowing from the fiery wonder of who God is. Can you imagine if Moses had been permitted to glimpse all of God's glory—full in the face?

God is holy. He is set apart from us as His created people. He is not a mere man, but holy, majestic, and wonderful beyond our comprehension.

He spoke the world into being. He breathed and it came to be. Earth, sky, land, water, plants, animals … all appeared by the hushed command of His voice. One word—and the form of all the earth. Another word—and the form was filled with beauty and intricacy and miraculous, complicated, functioning life. Only God can do that. Only God can create something from nothing. Out of the great void came life and beauty. Because He told it to. Psalm 33:6-8 says, "By the word of the Lord the heavens were made, and by the breath of his mouth all their host. He gathers the waters of the sea as a heap; he puts the deep in storehouses. Let all the earth fear the Lord; let all the inhabitants of the world stand in awe of him!"

We are meant to fear God. He is the one who set the earth spinning on its perfect orbit, the one who lit the skies with orbs of fire to illume the day and the night, the one who created hundreds of thousands of species of animals with bodies so detailed it takes libraries to explain their anatomy. He holds this great big world in His hands, and we are but dust.

The Bible tells us that one day every knee will bow before God, and every tongue will confess that He is Lord. Every single created being will one day offer worship in reverential fear (Romans 14:11).

We fear God because He is big. There are a host of long, theological words that describe God's character. He is omniscient and omnipresent. He is unchangeable, all-powerful, and just. He is utterly holy. He is over all, in all, and through all. He is the great I AM.

Here is the beautiful thing, though. Remember those two definitions of fear? We don't have to get stuck at the first definition. Unlike the demons. Unlike the Midianites. Unlike those who lived in Jericho. Our knees should knock together just a little when we behold who God is. We should bow and shake and turn our faces because His glory is blinding. But, if you are a believer—if your life has been entrusted to Christ and you have received the mercy He rained down at the cross—you don't have to keep trembling. At least not in a "Wow, He's really terrifying," kind of way.

Jesus, who shed His blood for you, has dropped to His own knees and covered you, shielded you. You are hidden in Christ. Tucked, like Moses, in the cleft of the Rock. Fear looks different from the safety of Jesus' arms.

I love the part in *The Lion, the Witch, and the Wardrobe* when the children ask the beavers whether the great lion, Aslan, is safe. "'Safe?' said Mr. Beaver. 'Don't you hear anything Mrs. Beaver tells you? Who said anything about safe? 'Course he isn't safe. But he's good.'"[2]

That is our God. He is big and powerful and uncontainable. But He is good. And so we fear Him, but that fear is nested within our trust in His goodness. Our fear of God is woven together with the awesome discovery that He loved us enough to die for us. He made Himself one of us in order to give His life for us. He makes Himself small enough every day to care about the intricate details of each and every one of our lives. He hears the prayers of His people and gives us His Holy Spirit to comfort us, to teach us, to empower our hearts and lives. The Word He inspired and preserved for us opens daily with fresh and unique insight for each of us—wherever and whoever we are. Our God is not only big and mighty; He is personal. He is *Yahweh* and He is *Abba*, our papa.

Dr. Edward T. Welch, in his book *When People are Big and God is Small*, speaks about the fear of the Lord as a continuum. On one end of the spectrum is terror and dread because of God's power, and at the other end is reverence, devotion, trust, and worship. If we are terrified of God, we want to hide from Him and His holy justice. But as we draw near to God, we learn of His deep love and we begin to trust and love Him in return. Raw fear knows only God's judgment, and flees. But fear with devotion knows God's judgment, and also His tender mercy.

Welch writes, "The Bible teaches that God's people are no longer driven by terror-fear, or fear that has to do with punishment. Instead, we are blessed with worship-fear, the reverential awe motivated more by love and the honor that is due Him." [3]

If our view of God is big, and our view of ourselves is small, if we are sheltered by the mercy of Jesus and our lives are hidden in His sacrifice so that we are no longer enemies of God, then we rightly fear God. And if we fear God as we are called to, we will revere His thoughts, His words, and His pleasure more than any earthly thing (or person!). Because He will be so great in our eyes that nothing can compare. We will delight to obey Him, and we will walk in the glorious freedom that comes from being utterly submitted to the Lord of our lives.

But if we forget to look up in awe, and we view ourselves as bigger than we are, if we think we can handle carrying that big bundle of weighty rubble, we entangle our hearts in the fear of man.

Just as the definition of the "fear of the Lord" encompasses a range of responses, so does the "fear of man." To quote Dr. Welch again, "The road leading to the fear of man may be expressed in terms of favoritism, wanting others to think well of you, fearing exposure by them, or being overwhelmed by their physical power."[4]

We can fear man in a variety of ways. The terrain you have traveled is different than the path I have walked along. But I would dare to suggest that even if you are confident, composed, and self-reliant, even if you have never felt a paralyzing longing to be approved of; you are carrying around a backpack filled with some form of man-fearing. Any time we shoulder an improper preoccupation with other people and their perceived power over us, we are fearing man.

If you find yourself showing favoritism to those who have achieved wealth or worldly success, you are fearing man.

If you find yourself hiding your faith in God from those who disagree with your beliefs, or if you clam up when opportunities to share the gospel arise, you are fearing man.

If you erect walls around yourself so others will see only a perfect exterior, while guarding your hidden sins and vulnerabilities, you are fearing man.

If you often follow the crowd in your decision making—for better or for worse—rather than seeking God's wisdom in the Bible, you are fearing man.

If you feel you have to accumulate the best of everything, to be up-to-the-minute in toys, technology, or clothing, you are fearing man.

Throughout this book, I will share personal stories about how I have allowed my own fear of what others think to control my thoughts and actions. Personally, I have struggled with exalting people over God, and fearing their thoughts and opinions of me more than I fear the God of the universe. I have cared far more about myself, and about pleasing other people, than I have cared about honoring and obeying God. In fact, I have cared more about *looking* like my life was glorifying God than about *actually* glorifying God.

Are you beginning to see how all of us have picked up this burden in some way, shape, or form? My knapsack of ungodly fear might be heavier than yours. In fact, I'm quite sure it is—or I wouldn't be compelled to write this book! Yet, each of us needs to look at ways to exalt our God and decrease our dependency on man's approval.

Before I move on, I want to touch briefly on the final category of man-fearing: the fear of being physically harmed or overpowered by other people. Here are some examples: domestic violence, sexual abuse, persecution, war. Christians in other countries often experience real, physical danger for professing their faith in Jesus. A soldier in war-time experiences the real, physical dangers of battle. A battered wife experiences real, physical danger from her husband.

Fear is natural and right in those situations. It is a God-given mechanism to keep us safe by propelling us to flee danger (or in some instances, to face danger for a cause bigger than ourselves).

But even a right and natural fear can slide down a slippery slope to an unhealthy and controlling fear of man—where we forget God's sovereignty and kindness and are utterly controlled by the person (or people) we fear. Fear that has a right place in our lives can easily escalate to an improper fear if we do not keep a right view of God at the forefront of our thinking.

If, in our fear of physical harm, we hold a high and holy view of the God who made us and loves us, if we cling to His promises and trust in His care of us, then we keep natural fear from becoming the fear of man. There are several biblical examples of men and women who rightly feared God even in dangerous situations, and we will look at some of them later.

This is obviously a topic we could dive deeply into, and I want to just glide the surface of these sometimes murky waters. As we talk about genuine fear of physical harm, especially in terms of people who have been victims of all kinds of abuse, a myriad of questions arise. Where is God, we wonder, when people hurt others in unspeakable ways? And how can we suggest that a victim of such harm might still hold to a trust in the goodness of God? How could God possibly seem "bigger" than the perpetrator when the perpetrator is real and present and threatening, and God is distant—or so it seems?

If this is your situation, I do not want to minimize the heartache you've experienced, or the difficulties in reconciling God's trustworthiness with your circumstances. For the purposes of this book, we are going to primarily address the fear of man that leads to favoritism, people-pleasing, and deep concern over how others perceive us. But, I do want to touch (incompletely, of course) on a biblical response to a genuine fear of physical harm.

God cares deeply about our hurts. He is the comforter of the broken. He is the God who sees. He knows, and He cares. In Scripture, Jesus reaches out to the widows, the needy, the lonely, and the victims. Christ Himself suffered in ways we cannot imagine when He bore our sins on the cross. He was rejected, ridiculed, abused, and despised. The crowds spat on Him. A crown of piercing thorns was placed on His head, and nails were driven through His flesh to hold His body to the tree. He understands your suffering. He allows suffering on our sin-broken world, but He never allows it to be wasted.

Romans 8:28 promises, "And we know that for those who love God all things work together for good, for those who are called according to his purpose."

Ultimately, for believers, the sadness of earth will be undone. Sally Lloyd-Jones, in the *Jesus Storybook Bible*, offers a paraphrase of parts of the book of Revelation for children. Writing about John's visions, she says,

One day, John knew, Heaven would come down and mend God's broken world and make it our true, perfect home once again.

And he knew, in some mysterious way that would be hard to explain, that everything was going to be more wonderful for having been so sad.

And he knew then that the ending of The Story was going to be so great, it would make all the sadness and tears and everything seem like just a shadow that is chased away by the morning sun.[5]

We are not just victims of earthly circumstances, we are victims of the unfathomable, beautiful, and eternal grace of our Lord Jesus Christ.

In the midst of whatever fears we face, God is to be trusted. He is to be revered. Whether our fears are related to horrifying circumstances or merely our own selfishness and pride (or perhaps both), God is bigger. He is loving, sovereign, and worthy of our trust in Him. He deserves our overarching, reverent awe of who He is and the story He is unfolding as He redeems His beloved.

Jeremiah 17:5 reads, "Cursed is the man who trusts in man and makes flesh his strength, whose heart turns away from the Lord." And verses 7-8 go on to say, "Blessed is the man who trusts in the Lord, whose trust is the Lord. He is like a tree planted by water, that sends out its roots by the stream, and does not fear when heat comes, for its leaves remain green, and is not anxious in the year of drought for it does not cease to bear fruit."

I don't know about you, but I want to live in faith and trust in the Lord. I want to fear God.

I don't come to this book with all the answers, or a ten-step formula to find freedom from the fear of man. I come to the writing of this book as a woman—a wife, a mama, and a daughter of the King—who longs to live for the glory of her Savior. I have been enslaved for too long to an inward-focus on myself and how others view me. I don't want my life to be about me anymore. I want it to be about Jesus, and about how I can serve and glorify Him as I allow His Spirit to en-grace my everyday life. Our lives are a part of the magnificent story He is writing. But when we are bonded to a fear of others, we miss out on what He is weaving all around us.

Will you join me on this journey? Let's explore the ways the fear of man causes us to stumble, and then search together for biblical answers to how we can shrug off that figurative weight.

CHAPTER TWO:
What's in Your Backpack?

Last week, our family returned from a trip to California to attend my grandfather's memorial service and celebrate his remarkable life. Because the drive to San Diego is seventeen hours (even without preschooler-spaced potty breaks) we took a few extra days and turned our travels into a vacation.

Have you ever packed a family of six into a car for a road trip? If you have, then you understand the preparation, planning, and just plain stuffing that go into such a feat. We were planning to camp overnight, so the back of the car was loaded with gear: sleeping bags, blow-up mattress pads, pillows, one monstrous green tent, a small stove to boil water, and flashlights. We filled a large cooler with food for picnics and snacks along the way. The portable crib was folded up and tucked in for our youngest daughter. The girls packed two to a suitcase, following an illustrated list Mommy had given them. At each seat, there was a favorite doll ready to be snuggled, a cozy blanket, and a spill-proof water bottle.

And then, there were the backpacks. One blue and gray, one purple plaid, one magenta, and a miniature one with pink polka dots for baby Hope. I gave my girls suggestions on how to fill their backpacks, but I didn't double check their choices the way I did the suitcases of clothes. I expected a few books, a notepad or coloring book, crayons, and their zippered pouches of souvenir money. What more did they need?

At some point, we had to shuffle the seating arrangements to make room for two cousins. I found myself clearing the space around my oldest daughter's seat. I could have used a shovel to remove all of the assorted trash and flowing backpack debris. A ball of now-tangled yarn had been unwound around her booster seat. At least six books were flayed about the area, and a torn paper bag had once held ten different doll outfits—all now scattered about the middle seat of our Suburban. Two pairs of socks were crumpled and inside out beneath the seat. Torn coloring pages were everywhere. As I shoved the mess and mayhem back into my sweet daughter's empty backpack, I marveled at how much she had managed to cram into the single child-sized cavity. I couldn't believe how much stuff was in her backpack.

In this chapter, I want us to shrug off our own knapsacks and sort through the accumulated junk we might be carrying with us in terms of man-fearing. We touched on a few aspects in the first chapter as we defined what the fear of man is, but now let's dive deeper. Let's look at the individual pieces of backpack debris, and identify them for what they really are. Like my daughter's overflowing purple plaid backpack, we might be surprised at everything we have managed to stuff in there!

Let's reach into the front pocket of our knapsacks and pull out a rumpled sock or two. One manifestation of fearing man is the fear of being exposed. It is the fear of having others see who we really are, including the messes, muddles, and mistakes we have made. We protectively guard our inner lives, fearful of how others might perceive us if they really knew us.

We could talk about masks; we could talk about walls. Both images apply to this fear, and don't all of us do it? Don't we hide—sometimes?

At the beginning of time, Adam and Eve walked with God in the cool of a beautiful garden. They plucked ripe fruit from tree branches shimmering with morning dew; they tasted the sweetness of provision from God's hand. They roamed, barefoot, naked, and safe through moist, loamy soil from which sprung plants of every genus and species. Their eyes drank in beauty unhindered—beauty unmarred by briars, thorns, or weeds. Every plant bloomed and flowered with lush, colorful beauty. The animals lived in peace. Lions and elephants—even dinosaurs—sank their feet deep into that same soil, and Adam called them by name without fear. God had fashioned Adam from the dust of the earth, then formed Eve from Adam's bones, and He cared for them utterly. Completely. Every need they had was met. Every joy in knowing God was theirs. He loved them, and they were His.

We cannot even imagine the breathtaking wonder of a world untouched by the devastation of sin, not yet ravaged by the consequences of disease, death, and destruction.

And then, the snake came. He slithered into the garden, pointed tongue flashing and beady eyes glinting in the sun. He spoke to Eve. His words—lies—enticed her. He persuaded her with crooked, conniving words, and she listened. She believed the lies. So, she ate the fruit. Adam was with her, and he, too, bit into the juicy flesh of the forbidden fruit.

In that one taste, everything shattered. The beauty of knowing God so intimately was tainted by the sin of disobeying Him. They looked down and saw, in shame, that they were naked. They had nothing with which to cover the truth of their wrongdoing. They were bare before the Lord. He knew their hearts, and now, He knew their sin. Genesis 3: 8-10 says, "And they heard the sound of the Lord God walking in the cool of the day, and the man and his wife hid themselves from the presence of the LORD God among the trees of the garden. But the LORD God called to the man and said to him, 'Where are you?' And he said, 'I heard the sound of you in the garden, and I was afraid, because I was naked, and I hid myself.'"

Certainly, nakedness itself was not the issue. Adam and Eve had shared the garden prior to the snake's intrusion, and they had lived together, unclothed, without shame. They had nothing to hide, and their intricately created bodies were beautiful. They were creatures fashioned in God's image, sharing life in the garden with each other and with Him, and they had nothing to be ashamed of.

But the fruit of the tree—the Tree of the Knowledge of Good and Evil—had slipped down their throats and filled their innermost beings with a slimy, shameful secret. They knew evil along with good, and it soiled their own hearts. They were dirty with sin. They could see it in each other, nakedness revealing the ugly truth of their heart transformation. They could see it in themselves. And they knew God could see it in them.

Adam and Eve hid from God. They were afraid to have their shame exposed before the one who had made them. But, of course, God already knew their sin.

Grieved by their sin and yet not taken by surprise—not wringing His mighty hands and wondering how to proceed with a back-up plan for living in relationship with His beloved—God responded with justice and mercy. He set His perfect rescue operation into motion as He chastised and punished the snake, then Eve, then Adam. He gently laid forth the consequences of their sin; He told them how their disobedience was unraveling the perfect beauty of their world, how ugliness had crept in to prickle plants with thistles, how pain would accompany the birth of their children, and how life would involve hard work, sweat, struggle, and death.

Then, with the same loving hands that had shaped each contour of their bodies, God covered them. He sewed them garments made of animal skin, and wrapped them in the tender grace of His covering. They had hidden from Him, and now He Himself hid them in clothing He made for them.

It's not a coincidence that God killed an animal to cover the shame and nakedness of Adam and Eve. He was foreshadowing the coming story. He sacrificed an animal to clothe His people on the day they left the garden, and He would one day sacrifice His Son to clothe His people in His righteousness.

God was so kind to Adam and Eve, and He is so kind to us.

Do you see what happened that day? When sin entered the world, so did shame. Just as Adam and Eve feared being exposed before God, so would they fear exposure by other people. They would look for ways to cover their shame. They would hide.

So do we. A part of receiving our redemption in Christ is seeing our own ugliness, isn't it? We have to grapple with the truth that we are sinners before the face of a holy God; we have to admit we are broken, messy, worm-like sinners squirming around in need of His merciful covering.

And, oh, how He covers us! He covers us with His blood. His love poured out at Calvary covers our depravity and presents us, miraculously, as His beautiful bride. The one He loves. He gives us a pure-white robe and clothes us in Jesus' own righteousness.

Yet, here on earth, we don't quite see that spotless robe of His covering, do we? We thank God for His grace and love, but we still squirm in our own sinful squalor as we struggle to live in the Spirit when our flesh yet hankers after selfishness.

We know who we are called to be, who we long to be, who we were made to be. But we look down and see the mud and muck of who we really are, and that's when we hide.

We are afraid of people witnessing our errors, noticing our mistakes, or uncovering our past (and present) sins.

I have never had a traffic violation of any kind. I tend to drive a mile or two under the speed limit, and every interaction I have ever had with a police officer has been friendly, cordial, and helpful. But, I am terrified of having a policeman catch me doing something wrong while I drive, even though I try desperately to do everything exactly right. Here's the embarrassing truth. I have sometimes (not often!) turned off a main road and taken an unnecessary detour in order to hide from a police officer who happened to appear in the road behind me. Driving in front of one makes me nervous. I don't want to mess up. I don't want to do anything wrong. And if I do, that uniformed officer has the power to expose me, to shame me. I can't bear that, so I hide.

Dr. Welch teaches that there are two kinds of shame-consciousness: shame that stems from our own sin and shame that results from painful victimization. Regardless of the back-story on our shame, "one reason we fear people is that they can expose or humiliate us."[6]

After the fall, "God could see our disgrace, and other people became a threat because they too could see it. Their perceived opinions could now dominate our lives. The story of Scripture quickly became one in which people frantically looked to hide and protect themselves from the gazes of God and other people."[7]

We carry with us a crushing shame over our own sin, and even as believers who know God's grace covers us, we often scurry to shield our messy selves from the scrutiny of others.

In Angie Smith's book, *What Women Fear*, she shares the stories of women who have written to her, sharing their fears of being found out. Some confessed overwhelming feelings of despair they kept hidden, others shared that their marriages were disintegrating behind a picture-perfect façade. Others questioned their own salvation even as they led Bible studies. Some stories were dramatic; others were seemingly minor. While the situations varied, the common and nearly universal thread was that all of us fear being known at the deepest level. We fear others seeing—knowing—our struggles. I fear being found out by you, while you fear being found out by me.

"If you are anything like me," Angie writes, "you can immediately think of several things you believe would ruin other people's perceptions of you. You might even say you spend more time presenting yourself rather than being present."[8]

Angie goes on to share, though, that most of us tend to be much more accepting of others' weaknesses than we think they will be with ours. I think she's right. We don't dwell on others' errors or struggles; we love people for who they are, and for the ways we see Christ in them—despite their muddles and mess-ups. We are content to see others as works-in-progress, as moving toward sanctification without being all the way there.

Yet we get hung up on our unworthiness and look for ways to patch up the holes, ways to hide the things about ourselves we don't like. We proudly display the polished veneer of our goodness, while whitewashing those areas we haven't quite figured out yet—those zones of our character that are still under construction.

Later, we will talk more about Christ's gracious covering of us. We will unpack the truth that who we believe we are in Christ—and who we believe others are in Christ—can actually change our desires to hide. The gospel of Christ completely intersects with our shame and our fear, and His robes of righteousness are truly enough. The gist, though, for now, is this: we are all packing around some smelly old socks. Our fear of exposure, our consciousness of our shame, is one of those.

Tucked in closely to the wrinkled socks is its companion fear: the fear of not measuring up. This is the aspect of man-fearing where we compare ourselves to others, concerned about whether we will be found worthy. We see the accomplishments, the possessions, the outward beauty, or even the Christian walk of another person and we sink deep inside ourselves, fearing that what we have to offer is simply not enough.

While this fear is closely related to the shame-fear that drives us to hide our true selves, it is not a fear of having our sins uncovered. It is, conversely, a fear that even our "good" is not "good enough."

This is the fear that propelled me, as a six-year-old, to stay in the classroom at recess so I could perfect my drawing of a rainbow. I liked my picture;

I thought it was lovely, until I glanced across the room and saw the brilliant beauty of Ana's artwork. Suddenly, my own masterpiece was not good enough. The standard had been raised, and I could not measure up. I could no longer garner the approval of my beloved teacher because my work was now merely second-rate.

Every year, at Christmastime, I eagerly await the flood of holiday letters that fill my mailbox. I tear open every crisp envelope to see the smiling faces of friends and family, all entwined and bordered with intricate Christmas-y designs and colors. I flip the pictures over and double-check the empty envelopes, hoping for a letter to go along with photo. And I read every word, swallowing those sweet morsels of friendship and longing to share life with old friends instead of just letters.

Yet, somewhere in the middle of reading those much-anticipated Christmas cards, I begin to feel small. Someone's three-year-old can read. A first-grader is playing Beethoven on the piano. The twelve year-old is captain of the lacrosse team and has a business selling homemade pottery. The baby has the state capitals memorized. A busy, hard-working dad just ran a marathon, and a stay-at-home mom is changing lives through her volunteer work. And there are no stains on those children's clothing in their professional-looking photograph.

As I read the beautiful letters from people I love, my spirits sort of sag. I am happy to know their families through the words on the page, and I am thankful for each success and joy they have experienced. But where are the letters that tell my story? The one that goes: "Every day of this year was marked by another stain on our carpet. We were messy! We are bumbling and imperfect and just trying to figure out how to live faithfully in the chaos that defines our days. My wonderful, beautiful daughters spent most of their time squabbling with one another, giving us lots of opportunities to explore together how the gospel can help us with our daily struggles to be kind. Our homeschool is usually a mess (and so is our girls' handwriting!), and sometimes I wonder if we are learning anything, but we always manage to share snuggles and a story on the couch. We didn't win any races, but we explored the wilderness together by foot, ski, bike, and canoe. Day-to-day life is not always easy, and we are all sinners, but we see God's grace daily. We pray that we are growing in Him as a family so we can display the beauty of His gospel through the messes and miracles of our lives."

I shrink back from writing my own Christmas letter after I have perused the stack of cards in my basket a few times. Our family is not really very special, it seems. We struggle more than we succeed. My letter would not be nearly as impressive as the ones I have read. I hide behind a simple greeting and a verse of Scripture, and I leave it at that.

The truth is, I probably could weave a pretty story on a page and print it out to fold neatly inside our Christmas card. But I don't want to erect a wall. I don't want to wear a mask. I don't want someone, like me, who is already feeling insecure about her own small life, to read my lightly enhanced version of Wachob-lore, and feel like she has to hide her reality because, when it is set against the backdrop of my family's picture-perfect card, it seems messy.

My husband graciously reminds me that behind every one of those seemingly perfect family photos and letters, there are kids who bicker, glasses of spilled milk, sleepless nights with screaming babies, and failed math tests. There are weary mommies who occasionally snap irritably at sinful children, and who sometimes leave the clean laundry in the basket for a week before putting it away. There are daddies who struggle to fit in exercise or Bible study with an already full schedule of work and parenting. No one is perfect.

I hope I continue to receive wonderful batches of Christmas cards every year. I delight in them! And, by their very nature, those cards are meant to share just the highlights. There is nothing wrong with sending a glowing picture of God's grace in your life. But if you want to add in a line or two about how you and your kids aren't perfect either … well, it would make me feel better!

We all try to put our best foot forward. As we have already mentioned, we all patch up the ugly holes in our veneer and try to look good. We airbrush. We hide.

Oftentimes, we do it because we fear that we will not measure up. We won't be good enough. We can't keep up with the endeavors, the assets, the appearance, or the character of others. We fear what they will think of us when we fail to meet the standard.

Do you have certain realms of your life where this fear bursts onto the scene?

A businessman works hard to scramble up the corporate ladder, logging late hours and infrequent days off, because he longs for his accomplishments to be approved of.

A teenager fights anger and envy because he looks around and sees his peers driving shiny new cars and pocketing the newest iPhones, while he rides the school-bus and taps out his texts on his dad's old flip phone that can't even take pictures.

A young woman scours fashion magazines and spends hours at the mall, finding clothes that match the newest trends. Every morning, she spends an hour in front of the mirror, styling her hair and applying make-up to achieve the fashionable look she desires.

A wife fusses and frets over her home, fearing it will never match the pictures in *House Beautiful*, or even be as lovely or perfectly clean as the neighbor's.

A stay-at-home mom listens to the fervent prayers of her friend. She watches her friend's uninhibited worship and hears the beautiful way she speaks of her relationship with her Savior. Feeling her own walk with the Lord lacks the fervor and sweetness she sees in her friend, she wonders whether she needs to spend two hours reading the Bible every day, rather than just one. What she's doing just doesn't seem to be enough.

The desire to be approved of and the fear that we won't measure up can infiltrate any aspect of our lives.

Personally, I identify much more with the latter two examples. That is my season of life, and those are the spheres where I am most often caught-off guard by the overwhelming feeling of smallness.

When it comes to gadgets and gear, I am perfectly content to stay behind the times with my flip-phone and my very muddy kiddo-mobile. When it comes to beauty, I am (most of the time) happy to don my same-old jeans and cardigans that magically morph into casual knee-length skirts and tees in the spring. I prefer to spend the quiet hour before my daughters wake up reading and praying, rather than fussing with a complicated hairstyle or makeup.

But I struggle with alternating pride and embarrassment over the state of my simple home. And I find myself feeling timid and inferior when I am surrounded by a group of other women, all of whom seem to be kinder, more organized, more accomplished, better mommies, wiser, more gracious, more in love with Jesus, and, yes, more beautiful than I am. In fact, I shy away from gatherings of women because I know my wayward heart will keep me up all night, numbering the countless ways I fall short.

Just as all of us have true sin in our hearts that needs the real covering of Jesus Christ, we all, too, need to recognize our smallness before the God who created the universe. There are deep truths in each of these fears, questions and needs that are meant to be answered and met in Christ alone. But we humans warp our God-needs by asking other humans to meet them. We fear man instead of God, and we spend our lives hiding, grasping, and straining to feel enough.

We are not enough. We can't meet the standard. God laid out His perfect standard in the Old Testament books of the law. And His people failed miserably at keeping His commands. The standard is high, and not one of us can reach it. We can't grasp or strain or stand on tip toes. It is impossible to earn God's favor by our good works.

Can you agree with that? There is a standard. And we cannot, despite our best efforts, measure up to it. Romans 3:23 reminds us, "for all have sinned and fall short of the glory of God."

We all fall short! None of us measures up.

Except Jesus Christ.

Galatians 3:24 says, "So then, the law was our guardian until Christ came, in order that we might be justified by faith."

When Jesus walked on earth, He fulfilled every aspect of the law on our behalf. He met every requirement. He never sinned in word, in thought, or in deed. He defeated every temptation that assaulted Him. He kept every command of God the Father as He lived in perfect communion with Him.

Then, in grace and mercy we cannot fully comprehend, God heaped the ugliness of our sin upon Jesus' sinless frame. Jesus carried the foul stench of broken humanity to the cross, and He paid for it. He took the punishment we deserved; He was severed from His Father as God turned His face from the wretchedness of our sin and poured His righteous wrath on the Son He loved.

And in a heavenly transaction that was both horrendous and beautiful, He took our now-atoned for sin and handed us His perfect record.

"There is therefore now no condemnation for those who are in Christ Jesus. For the law of the Spirit of life has set you free in Christ Jesus from the law of sin and death. For God has done what the law, weakened by flesh, could not do. By sending his own Son, in the likeness of sinful flesh and for sin, he condemned sins in the flesh, in order that the righteous requirement of the law might be fulfilled in us, who walk not according to the flesh but according to the Spirit" (Romans 8: 1-4).

When we could accomplish nothing, Christ accomplished everything. Everything we could not do, Christ did for us.

Justification is a big, theological term. A beautiful, splendid, wondrous theological term that crowns believers with hope and joy because of Jesus' life, death and resurrection. Elyse Fitzpatrick defines justification beautifully in her book, *Found in Him*:

> *Justification means 'just as if I never sinned,' and that's exactly how God the Father looks at us. When he sees us, he is happy that we are betrothed to his Son, for he has cast all our sin out of his sight so it's as if we had never sinned. I am, all who believe are, perfect in his sight. That's almost too good to be true, isn't it? We're that forgiven? Our reputation is that clean? 'Behold the Lamb of God who takes away the sin of the world!' (John 1:29) Atonement for your sin has already been made. God no longer sees it; he no longer holds it against you. Jesus has done this!*[9]

But justification doesn't stop with this glorious redemption from our sin. When we were justified by faith in Jesus Christ, through His cleansing blood, we were also given the record of His pure, good works. You know how our earthly good works are often marred by impure motives or selfish attitudes? Jesus' good works were truly good. And they are credited to us! Elyse Fitzpatrick goes on to say:

> *Not only has God forgiven all our sins and erased the record of our wrongdoing so that he no longer sees it, but he also added to that clean record a list of all the good works Jesus did as he lived for about thirty-three-and-a-half years, perfectly fulfilling the law's demands in our place. In other words, just as the first part of our definition is, 'Just as if I had never sinned,' this second part is, 'Just as if I had always obeyed.' Think of that. Not only are you forgiven; you've been blessed with a reputation and record*

that proclaims you've always done everything you were supposed to![10]

We can't measure up. We can't be good. As I gently told my daughter this morning when her behavior called for discipline, all of us have ugly hearts filled with sin and selfishness. We all need Jesus! His perfect life, His atoning death, and His magnificent resurrection are the only hope we have of standing unafraid before our holy and just God. By His grace, He washes away our sin and we come, unashamed and dressed in the white robes of Jesus' righteousness. We are not enough. But He is.

We are right to feel small before our fearsome, wonderful, and incredibly merciful God.

But, as author Emily P. Freeman points out, "There is a difference between embracing your smallness in the presence of Christ, and feeling like a nobody in the presence of others."[11]

The difference is the fear of man.

Unzip the side pocket of your backpack with me. Pull out what you find and hold it up to the light. A tangled knot of pink yarn? A wrinkled page filled with penciled doodles?

Our next area of man-fearing is, again, closely related to the previous two. Sometimes, we are not necessarily afraid of having our sin revealed, or of being "less than." We are just afraid of standing out. We are afraid of being different.

This is the peer pressure felt by a teenager when "everyone else is doing it," or wearing it, or saying it. This is the child who is sucked into wrong behavior because a throng of other children "started it."

And, you know what? This peer pressure sort of man-fear may not always lead us to make overtly wrong choices. It may be a perfectly good choice, but we make it for the wrong reasons. It may be a choice between two neutral things, but we ignore the Lord's tug on our own hearts and instead follow the crowd.

It may be that we allow our hearts and minds to be overcome with the fear of man in a situation where our differences seemingly make us stand out.

A few years ago, our family was enjoying a reunion with extended family. A warm summer evening included a dressy dinner party to celebrate my grandpa's one-hundredth birthday. I was seven months pregnant with our fourth daughter, and my clothing options were limited. I finally settled on a comfortable cotton sundress, and slipped my swollen feet into flip flops. I live in Wyoming, and dressing up usually means wearing your cleanest jeans and maybe tucking in your shirt. It never occurred to me that my choice of footwear would be inappropriate for a formal(ish) gathering.

We arrived at the restaurant, and I immediately became aware of how much better-dressed the other women were. My jewelry (nothing except my wedding ring), my hair (simply clipped back from my face), and my clothes were all wrong. And my shoes! I was the only woman in attendance who was not wearing heels.

Throughout the dinner, I was painfully self-conscious of my girlish cotton dress and sandals. I felt like I stood out. And maybe I did.

But, did it matter? Nope. It really didn't. I should have laughed a little at my country bumpkin ways, thanked the Lord that I didn't have to stuff my poor pregnant feet into heels, and turned my attention to enjoying and blessing the people around me. My self-focus and fear of standing out hindered me from glorifying the Lord in my interactions that night.

The fear of man turns our focus inward. It makes us worry about what others will think. Will they think I am weird? That I don't belong? That I don't fit in?

The high school student at the party wonders if he will lose all his friends if he is the only one who doesn't drink.

A visitor to the church wonders whether she will be rejected if she raises her hands in worship. No one else seems to be expressing praise to God in that way.

I look down at my flip flops and cringe because no one else wore sandals to the dinner.

We all have felt awkward and alone because of something about us that stood out as being different or weird. And we have all based decisions (for better or for worse) on the fear of experiencing that awkward aloneness.

As believers, we *are* different. We do stand out. We are supposed to, at least in some ways. We have been reborn in Christ, risen to new life with Him, and because of Christ in us, we are fundamentally different beings than those who have not believed.

The new life blooming in our hearts as the Holy Spirit lives and works in us ought to manifest itself in choices, behaviors, and priorities that are set apart from the majority culture. Those differences ought not to be displayed in a manner that draws attention to the choices or behaviors themselves, as though we are better than unbelievers, but in such a way that Christ is glorified as the redeemer, the heart-changer, and the giver of life.

As a twenty-three-year-old working night shift in a children's hospital, I stood out from my fellow nurses (at least most of them) because I was engaged to be married, and had never shared a bed with my fiancé. Our commitment to purity made us appear strange in the eyes of our peers, but it also provided a platform to share how our love for Jesus impacted our life decisions.

My sister, a beautiful, tall, and gentle-speaking blonde who recently turned thirty, stands out in a crowd. She lives in South Korea, so in a sea of dark hair and eyes, her physical features make her stand out quite literally. But, it is her sparkly eyes and gracious smile that truly set Michelle apart. She loves Jesus deeply and fervently, and it shows in her everyday life. She is a vessel poured out for His service, washing the feet of the Korean teenagers she teaches in an international school near Seoul. She is passionate about reaching their hearts for Jesus, and her love for them is sincere, sacrificial, and beautiful. She stands out because she has surrendered her life to Jesus, and her life is built upon serving Him. She isn't normal! She is set-apart.

As Christians, we are called to the set-apart life. 2 Timothy 2:21 says, "Therefore, if anyone cleanses himself from what is dishonorable, he will be a vessel for honorable use, set apart as holy, useful to the master of the house, ready for every good work."

In Philippians, Paul tells believers, "Do all things without grumbling or questioning, that you may be blameless and innocent, children of God without blemish in the midst of a crooked and twisted generation, among whom you shine as lights in the world ..." (Phil 2:14-15).

And in the Sermon on the Mount, Jesus calls his followers to be lights. "You are the light of the world. A city set on a hill cannot be hidden. Nor do people light a lamp and put it under a basket, but on a stand, and it gives light to all in the house. In the same way, let your light shine before others, so that they may see your good works and give glory to your Father who is in heaven" (Matthew 5:14-16).

Our lives, our differences, ought to call attention to Christ, bringing Him glory for what He has done.

Different is good.

When we get caught up in a desire to blend in, to not stand out, we focus wrongly on one of two things. We are each unique creations, with genuine, beautiful differences in both our physical attributes and our personalities. Sometimes we are afraid of showing those small differences because we fear standing out in a crowd. Or, we are fearful of embracing our differentness as Christ-followers, and so we choose to pattern our lives after the world's design. We don't really want to be lights.

Either way, we are fearing man.

How about favoritism? How does that one fit in?

James 2:1 says, "My brothers, show no partiality as you hold the faith in our Lord Jesus Christ, the Lord of glory."

We can fear man by paying special attention to someone because of their perceived power, wealth, or influence. If we think a person has something to offer us, we may pander to them in order to increase our chances of their bestowing those offerings on us. Or, even without hoping for some sort of gift from an influential person, we may modify our behavior or show special favor simply because we especially care about what they will think of us.

This is not how Jesus lived, is it? During Jesus' time on earth, He reached out to those who had nothing to offer Him in return. He offered living water to a woman with a sordid past. He healed the sick and broken, the beggars, and the blind. He dined with outcasts, and travelled with a raggedy band of devoted fisherman and humble tradesmen. He showed no partiality to the rich or the powerful.

But we do.

The summer before my wedding, I went on a three-week mission trip to Panama, with Focus on the Family's *Brio* magazine. There were five hundred people with our group, and I co-led a team of about twenty teenage girls. The trip was safe, the accommodations were lovely, and our times of praise and worship were led by a fantastic band—or sometimes a famous Christian musician who came to bless the girls with a concert. It wasn't a difficult trip; we were not roughing it. But the sweet young girls who raised support for the trip poured their little hearts out in ministry, through drama, testimony, and lots of sticky hugs to beautiful Panamanian children.

One of the girls on my team was the younger sister of a well-known Christian musician—one of my favorite female musicians, actually. It was rumored that the older sister might join us for the last few days of our trip, and I found myself struggling. I struggled not to show special favoritism to this young girl because I hoped to be noticed by her older sister. It seems so silly now, but I wanted a chance to meet her sister, and it was a heart struggle to not be aware of that opportunity as I guided the young girl through ministry. The girl was the youngest teen on the trip, and she truly did need some extra attention and care from her leaders. And, for some reason, she latched on to me. But, I had to wrestle with my heart motives—to love her for who she was, without thinking of her famous sister.

Does that make sense? The funny thing is that the sister did come. And she was so unassuming, so unpretentious. Her heart for serving the girls was absolutely beautiful. It didn't take long for me to realize that I was wrong to want to know her because she was famous. Instead, I wanted to know her because she was a set-apart, whole-hearted servant of Jesus.

We are called to impartiality as believers, aren't we? Galatians 3:26-28 says, "For in Christ Jesus you are all sons of God, through faith. For as many of you as were baptized into Christ have put on Christ. There is neither Jew nor Greek, there is neither slave nor free, there is no male or female, for you are all one in Christ Jesus."

We warp our unity in Christ by applying worldly standards of success and measuring worth by the wrong yardstick. We show favoritism where there ought to be none.

Because, as you might guess, we fear man instead of God.

As you gather up the pieces of shrapnel from our backpack explosion, turn them over in your hands and really look at them.

Maybe, like me, you have wondered why it matters whether we live in fear of man or in fear of God. If a fear of man restrains our behavior, motivates us to success, or compels us to pursue goodness, then what is wrong with it? Why is it a problem? Why is it a sin?

Let's slip those heavy bundles back on for a moment—see how heavy and burdensome they feel. In the next chapter, we will wrestle under their load and sort out some of the ways a wrong view of God and man hinders our walks with the Lord and muddles our everyday lives.

CHAPTER THREE:
Crouched Low and Weighed Down

Home for a three-month break after our sophomore years of college, my future husband and I both volunteered to help with our church's youth group for the summer term. I had long-harbored a secret crush on tall, handsome Erik, and I will admit that his participation swayed my interest in volunteering.

In late July, our fearless youth leader, Andy, decided to take the group of teens on a backpack trip. Hardy, wilderness savvy explorers (like Erik) and less-experienced, brave-hearted tagalongs (like me) teamed up to trek up mountains and swim in alpine lakes. It was a wonderful trip.

At some point, I think Erik finally noticed me. A little. I think he had expected me to be girlish and wimpy about the less-glamorous aspects of camping, and my enjoyment of the outdoors impressed his wild adventurer sensibilities. Or maybe not. Maybe I was just the only person his age on the trip, and he was bored.

Either way, by the third day, he had started to flirt just a little. To tease and cajole and pester. And like a nineteen-year-old girl, I received his teasing open and giddy, treasuring his every word and collecting his attention in a hidden pocket of my young heart.

It was the final day of our adventure, so our backpacks should have been lighter than before. We had eaten most of our food, and the downhill hike should have felt easy. But all of a sudden, I felt weighed down. My backpack seemed heavy. My legs felt like lead.

For an hour I pushed through, gritting my teeth. Then, we stopped in the shade for a snack. As I flipped open the top of my backpack to retrieve a granola bar and water bottle, my hands hit something hard. Something really hard. A rock. A big rock. A ten pound boulder had been shoved into the top of my pack.

Naively, I pulled the rock out and looked around. Who had put a rock in my backpack?

My big, goofy crush was guffawing into his hands.

Still chortling, he confessed to hiding the rock there at our previous stop. He had never expected me to hike so far with it, he laughed.

I laughed, too. I was happy to leave the gray weight beneath the tree and skip on down the trail with a much-lightened pack. And I was happy for an excuse to punch Erik in the arm and give him a good-natured hard time about the practical joke he had played.

Just for the record, it took another two and a half years and a trip to the other side of the world before Erik really noticed me and began to pursue my heart. But that's another story.

I carried an extra ten pounds in my pack that day, physically aware of the strain, but totally ignorant as to why my load was so heavy. My enjoyment of the hike was affected by the added weight, and it was not until the rock was removed that I realized how blissfully freeing it was to walk light.

That's how it is when we carry around the weight of man-fearing, too. We struggle and strain beneath an unnecessary burden, but we don't necessarily understand how or why it is weighing us down.

How does a fear of man affect our daily lives? How does it hinder our walks with the Lord? Our relationships with others? Our ministries?

When we hoist the fear of man onto our shoulders, the burden of pleasing people presses us down into ourselves, preventing us from living, loving, and serving.

In our first year of homeschooling, my girls and I worked through parts of the first catechism, answering simple theological questions with memorized responses.

"Who made you?" I would ask. Sweet, high voices would chorus, "God!"

"Why did God make you and all things?" "For His own glory," they would reply.

"How can you glorify God?" And they would say, "By loving Him and doing what He commands."

Mankind was created to bring glory to God. He made us for His glory.

Did you catch that? We were made to bring glory to our creator. We were not made to bring glory or fame or honor to ourselves.

Like the moon, which reflects the light of the sun in order to illumine the night, we are mere reflections of God with no light of our own.

Fearing man can trap us into a mindset that says it is not enough to bring God glory. We think we need a bit of glory for ourselves, and we begin to care more about what people think than about what our Lord thinks.

Essentially, we miss the whole point of our existence. We bypass our ultimate purpose as created beings, and we grab hold of a wrong pursuit instead. We don't want to just glorify God; we want to be esteemed by man.

What does it mean to glorify God? John Piper defines it as "feeling and thinking and acting in ways that reflect His greatness, that make much of God, that give evidence of the supreme greatness of all His attributes and the all-satisfying beauty of His manifold graciousness."[12]

It's not about us, is it? We are intended to live our lives abandoned to Christ, concerned only about making His name great in all that we do and say. Our actions ought to point people to the gospel of grace.

But we don't always want to reflect His greatness or make much of God. Because we fear people more than God, we want them to make much of *us*.

The supreme joy of living *in* Christ and *for* His glory is lost in a mess of man-fearing. And we miss out. Hunkered down because of the rocks in our backpacks, our lives are hindered in a multitude of ways.

When we idolize the approval of others, we are hindered in our ability to serve.

For four years, I have directed the Cubbies portion of our church's AWANA ministry. AWANA is a wonderful Bible memory program for children, and Cubbies is the preschool component. I delight in my rowdy three and four-year-olds. I love their wiggles and their grins and the way they trip over their little feet when the run. I love how they don't quite get the game Duck, Duck, Goose, but they play it whole-heartedly anyway. I love how they wave their pudgy fingers in the air when they want to answer a question, and I love it when they remember a biblical truth I taught them the week before. I am never happier than when I am bent low, eye-to-eye with a child, sharing with them how much their great God loves them.

The Cubbies room is my place to serve in our local church, alongside other wonderful, faithful volunteers. I don't think I will budge from that spot unless someone forcefully boots me from it. When I am with those sweet kiddos, I know that I am where I'm supposed to be: wiping spilled juice, doling out Goldfish crackers, helping small hands color, and teaching from God's Word.

Sometimes, though, a parent stays to help. Or I have to recruit a new volunteer, someone I feel uncomfortable with or inferior to. And I find myself nervous, threatened, and fearful. What if she doesn't think I am doing a good job? What if he finds fault with my message? Or my methods? What if she thinks I am unskilled at the job I feel I have been called to do? What if he thinks he could run the ministry better than I can?

In those moments of self-doubt, I find I am unable to give myself fully to my blue-vested Cubbies. Instead of looking at their shining, peanut butter smeared faces as I teach, I am watching the grown-ups. I am wondering what the adults think, rather than praying for the hearts of the little ones and directing my teaching completely to their ears. I shape what I say around what I think the grown-ups want to hear. I worry that they are judging me and finding me inept.

Fearing man weighs us down in ministry. It keeps us from serving the Lord the way we are designed to—with our gazes focused solely on Him. Colossians 3: 17 says, "And whatever you do, in word or deed, do everything in the name of the Lord Jesus, giving thanks to God the Father through Him."

We aren't supposed to be constantly worrying about how others perceive the work we do unto the Lord.

Does it matter what others think? Of course it does. If my pastor, a wise shepherd whose calling is to lead and care for our church body, visited my classroom and sensed something was amiss in my teaching, it would matter greatly. He would be bound to address the issue, even to remove me from that role.

As I serve and love those children, though, I am supposed to keep my eyes on Jesus. My hands, my feet, my voice … they are His! If I teach and serve because I love Jesus, because I am in love with Him and in awe of His grace, it will look much different than if I serve out of a longing for man's approval.

I will not be offended by someone's "better ideas" for my classroom. I will be grateful for their input and unconcerned with whether I am small in their eyes.

My ministry will come from a pure, open heart. I will love those precious children as Jesus does. Serving them will not be a means for others to think well of me; it will be a natural overflow of the love I have received from Christ.

It will not matter whether I have the perfect resume, the right personality, or the optimal educational background for teaching preschoolers. If I am serving Christ alone, in the capacity He has called me to, He will equip me. I can trust Him as I unfurl my hands and my heart to allow His Spirit to work and love through my frailty.

When God called Moses to lead His people out of Israel, Moses balked. He feared what the Israelites would think of him, and he feared Pharaoh. How could he handle political negotiations with the king if he stammered and stuttered through his explanations? He wasn't sure he could trust His God to overcome his limitations or work through his inadequacies. Repeatedly, he questioned God, fearful of whether he would be accepted as a leader given his disabilities, his weaknesses, and his past. He feared man.

Yet God had chosen him, and with great kindness, He nudged Moses beyond his fears, gave him a spokesman to make up for his ineloquence, and used him in a powerful way to rescue His people.

Fearing people, we crouch low, unusable. Fearing God, we stand tall, open vessels for God to consecrate for His purposes.

⬦

Fearing man can also hinder us from worshipping the Lord.

Have you ever stood in church as the band plays, trying to worship, but utterly distracted? You notice an orange juice stain on your blouse and realize you never put on mascara. Your hair is still wet from a rushed morning shower, and the kids are a squabbling mess beside you. What must people think? How come everyone else seems to have it all together?

Or maybe your heart is stirred by the words of the song, and you ache to worship God with abandon—to sing loud and dance free. But you hold back. Because you don't want to stand out or look weird among the soft-singing, staid crowd of worshippers.

Maybe you aren't in church. Maybe you are hiking in the woods and the beauty of a mountain lake dappled with afternoon sunshine takes your breath away. Maybe everything in you wants to praise the Lord—aloud—for His creativity and His awesome handiwork. But everyone else is talking about the weather, and that would be awkward.

Walk with me back in time a little. Let's go visit a woman in a town called Bethany. This woman knew what it meant to lay aside the fear of man and truly worship Jesus. And her story is recorded in Scripture so we might catch a glimpse of radical, God-focused, and heartfelt worship.

In the pale morning light, Mary wrapped her robes tighter over her arms. A cool breeze rippled down the hills and she shivered. She had left the house early to pray, to watch the morning sun tiptoe up the eastern horizon. The sunrise was fading now, but the climbing ball of light had left crumbs of pink and orange clouds in its wake, and Mary tilted her face upward to give thanks for such beauty.

She had learned to seek the Lord first each day. The Master Himself had taught her that the worship of God was more important than anything else that fought for her attention. When she had sat at His feet while Martha bustled in the kitchen and demanded her help, Jesus had gently—oh, so gently—corrected Martha, and told Mary to continue listening. Mary remembered His words.

The work of the day awaited. She knew that even as she busied her hands with the making of bread, the cleaning, or carrying heavy jugs of water, she could still worship. She could still pray. Her conversation with the Lord didn't need to end simply because Lazarus had awoken and was hungry for his breakfast. And yet, this morning hour, while the town of Bethany lingered in sleepy quiet, and even bustling Jerusalem on the hillside above had yet to fully awaken, was precious to Mary.

Something was happening. As she prayed, she sensed the Lord revealing Himself to her. Since the day Jesus had told Lazarus to come forth from the musty tomb where he had lain dead for four days, many more had followed Jesus. They had seen His miracles, heard His powerful testimony and His wonderful teaching, and they had believed. But Mary knew that underneath the current of excitement and expectation carrying Jesus' followers, there was another current running. It was a swift flowing river of hatred and anger propelled by the Pharisees and leaders who saw Jesus as a threat.

Jesus Himself had prophesied of what was to come. He had warned them that He had come to lay down His life. Mary wasn't sure the disciples listened when Jesus said things like that. They still hoped He was going to lead them in a revolution, one that would free Israel from Roman rule. But Mary sensed that God's plan was different. Rumblings came from Jerusalem that the priests and Pharisees wanted to kill Jesus. The very thought sent another chill down Mary's spine.

She didn't fully understand Jesus' plan. But she believed that He was, indeed, the Messiah she had longed to see.

As Mary returned to the house, Martha hurried to greet her. "Mary! Jesus is returning. We must make preparations! Simon has asked us to prepare and serve the meal at his home. Hurry!"

Jesus! Mary's heart leapt. He would be here again. Tonight!

For the rest of the day, Mary worked diligently beside her sister, preparing food for the gathering. Her heart fluttered constantly within her chest as she thought of Jesus, wondering what truths He might teach them tonight, and wondering what was in store for her beloved Master in the days to come.

Finally, it was evening. Martha bustled to serve, fulfilling the role she loved, and excelled at. Mary listened to her instructions and worked busily alongside her, but she kept stealing glances at the Master. She hung on His every word, even as she scurried to replenish platters of food and clear empty dishes from the table.

Mary's devotion to Jesus swelled within her as she watched Him, as she listened to His gentle teaching. Jesus was the Son of God. And He sat here with them, reclining at Simon's table, partaking of food she had prepared, loving them. She was amazed at who He was.

She yearned to show Him her adoration, to show Him she loved Him and would follow Him—and His Father—until the end of her life. She wanted to comfort Him and somehow give Him strength for whatever lied ahead. She didn't know how to demonstrate those things, though. Especially on this night, when the disciples and other men gathered close to Jesus. What could she do?

Then Mary remembered the flask. The jar of purest nard was her only possession of monetary value, the only item she owned that was truly worth anything. Might she offer it to Jesus?

She bit her lip, pondering how such a gift might be received. She knew the others might not understand. Martha would question the wastefulness of pouring nard at the feet of Jesus. So would the disciples. They would think that she was crazy. They would watch her and they would scorn her offering. Somehow, though, Mary was certain Jesus would understand her intent.

She wrapped her shawls back around her shoulders and slipped out the door. Hurrying home, she found the flask on the shelf and tucked it beneath the folds of her garments. Her breath came ragged as she shuffled briskly through the street.

Mary entered the room and found Jesus still reclining at the table. She tread softly across the floor to Him and knelt humbly at His feet. She broke the flask and the rich scent of nard wafted through the air. She poured the costly oil over His head, and then His feet. She watched the ointment drip over his toes and she leaned lower, unbinding her hair. She let the locks of hair fall loose and began to wipe his feet tenderly with the dark strands.

She moved slowly, giving Jesus her heart as she worshiped Him in quiet adoration.

When she rose, Jesus smiled.

Judas, one of the disciples, snarled in her direction. "Why this waste? For this could have been sold for a large sum and given to the poor" (Matthew 26:8-9).

Mary held her breath. It was the question she had expected. The one she had feared. She lowered her gaze, her cheeks blushing crimson.

But Jesus said, with his kind firmness, "Leave her alone. Why do you trouble the woman? For she has done a beautiful thing to me. For you always have the poor with you, but you will not always have me. In pouring this ointment on my body, she has done it to prepare me for burial. Truly, I say to you, wherever this gospel is proclaimed in the whole world, what she has done will also be told in memory of her" (Matthew 26:10-13).

Don't you love that? Mary worshiped Jesus whole-heartedly. She chose to set aside the fear of man, and to revere God alone. She broke the flask of nard, poured it over His body, and adored Him in a way that made no sense to those around her. She risked their rejection, their scoffing, and their anger. And Jesus received her gift. In fact, He allowed her heartfelt offering of worship to become a beautiful example for every believer to come after her. He included her story in His word for us to learn from.

All because she worshiped God without fearing man.

I think of the precious example we would have missed out on if Mary had succumbed to doubt and fear in that moment. Her offering became an anointing, a preparation for burial. God used her in a way she would never have expected, simply because she followed His leading to worship in her own unique and beautiful way.

Let's throw off the fear of man and worship God with the abandon of Mary of Bethany.

Fearing man can stunt our relationships. When we fear others, we can't love them purely, unselfishly. We are constantly thinking of what they think of us, and so the opportunity for genuine relationship is thwarted by our twisted motives. We aren't able to put our whole focus and attention on someone else, because we are busy wondering what their perceptions of us are. In the midst of our feeble attempts to love, serve, and listen to others, we find ourselves frustrated by our inability to truly care about just them. We cannot be fully present with another person without shedding our preoccupation with ourselves. We want to be helpful, but we want them to notice our helpfulness. We want to be kind, and we want them to be aware of our kindness. It gets messy.

Emily P. Freeman shares an example of how this has played out in her life:

> *A friend shares a difficult struggle. Tears well up in her eyes as she talks. The pain runs deep, maybe more than she*

even knows. I'm aware of my desire to be helpful, to make
it better, to offer some words of hope. As I listen to my own
discomfort because of my inability to help her, I realize I
am thinking more of me than of her. Is it possible to stay
my attention on the person I'm with more that perseverate
on what my response will be to her? Is it possible to do just
one thing at a time?[13]

As Emily prayed about her mixed motives in this situation, she found that, indeed, such a thing was possible. "The earlier question *how can I help her?* is changing into a new question, *how can I see her?* How will Immanuel show himself right now, not just for her in her pain but for me in my self-obsession? *God with us* is big enough to handle us both."[14]

Have you ever felt that tug of war on your heart in the middle of a conversation? The desire to be the hands and feet of Christ to another, all the while wrestling with an inordinate fear of what she will think of you as you serve her? The desire to listen and know and love, juxtaposed against the fear of whether they will think you compassionate, find your words profound, *see* Jesus in you?

Somehow, we have to let go of our fear of others. In fearing God alone, we will actually become more like Him, and our service, our speech, and our love will all become more like His. We have to stop clinging to the desire to be *seen* as Christ-like so that we can actually *become* Christ-like. We have to stop worrying about what the other person thinks so we can enter into an unbroken relationship with them.

We also have to stop worrying about what the other person thinks so we can honestly share the love of Christ with her. If the Holy Spirit prompts us to share the gospel with another person, and we guard our fearful hearts by holding back the truth of salvation because we don't want to be rejected, we let a fear of man prevent us from our calling as believers: to know Christ and make Him known! We can't truthfully, openly, willingly share Jesus' love if we fear others. Evangelists and missionaries cannot be man-fearers. They must be God-fearers who love others *through* Christ.

Fearing man also takes a toll on our relationships because it keeps us from being vulnerable. We don't want others to see the miry places, do we? We hold ourselves back because we fear what they might think.

There was a period of motherhood, when my oldest was about three and my second daughter was a year old, when I found any excuse to turn down an invitation to a party or play-date. My sweet oldest has a feisty bent to her beautiful personality, and during that season she was difficult to reign in. It seemed that crowds of children brought out a wildness in her little heart, an excitement that often manifested itself in rough-housing, hitting, and general mayhem. We would gather with other mamas and kiddos, and a scream would erupt from the children's play. I would know my girl had caused the scream. Repeatedly, another child would run in, screaming that Elisa had done something to hurt him. I would find my daughter, sit with her, correct her behavior, and, after repeated cycles, skulk home, defeated, embarrassed, and sad. Finally, I decided I was done. I was trying so hard to be a good mommy, and my strong-willed, strong-hearted girl was pretty resistant to my training. I just knew those other mamas, the ones with the compliant, quiet children, were talking behind my back about what a horrible mom I was. I was afraid to be vulnerable, afraid to let them see my struggles. So I gave up. I hid in my house with my babies and my excuses.

It's sad to look back and realize that I missed opportunities for fellowship, opportunities to disciple my little one, and opportunities to be open and honest with mommies who might just have had wisdom or encouragement to share.

My bundle of wild exuberance was not mean-spirited. She was just rough, bigger than most of her playmates, and a bit rambunctious. She needed me to be patient with her, to love her for her God-given uniqueness, and train her in ways to corral her energies. Not to shrink back from fellowship and play so that I could hide our out-of-the-box parenting moments from my "perfect" mommy friends.

Have you ever let a fear of man hinder the growth of a relationship? Can you look back and see ways you have loved incompletely because your fear of the person's opinion kept you at arm's length? Do you long to love like Jesus—fully attentive, unconditionally, generously—but self preoccupation gets in the way?

I know I have, I can, and oh, I do!

An undue fear of man also cripples our decision-making skills.

Stifled decision-making can manifest in two forms. One is peer pressure—following the crowd into sinful decisions and unbiblical lifestyle choices. The other comes when we navigate our freedom in Christ, within biblical boundaries, by following others rather than seeking the Lord. We may ignore the Lord's prompting to follow Him in a certain direction because the majority of our fellow believers are headed the opposite way.

A believer can be lured to sin because he fears the approval of the mainstream culture. We dabble and toy with wrong behavior so we can be accepted. And as we do so, as we lose the peer pressure battle, our hearts wander far from God. We don't fear Him, and we aren't obeying Him.

We can also bypass the Lord's best for us by making choices that are good but are not best for us as individuals. We may quench the Spirit's nudging within our hearts and simply go the way of our Christian culture.

One area where I have struggled deeply with God-centered decision-making is in the realm of parenting. There are strong, loud voices within Christianity that promote certain, strict methods of raising our children. And while their insights are helpful, there is a tremendous problem in that those methods are taught as God's way, the biblical way. Frankly, the

Bible isn't that clear, and we parents have great freedom in leaning into the Lord as we love and train our unique blessings.

Can I share with you a snapshot of my first months as a new mama, struggling to shut out the external voices and just listen to Jesus?

With gritted determination, I backed out of the nursery, closing the door behind me. No sooner had the door shut than the crying began. Soft at first, a hesitant whimper of confusion, the cries escalated until our nine-hundred square foot cabin shuddered from the bellows of my tiny Elisa.

I sat on the edge of the couch, watching the clock. How many minutes had the book said? My baby girl cried on. After two-and-a-half minutes, I raced to the tiny bedroom, gathered her in my arms and snuggled her tight against my chest. I just couldn't do it! Finally, Elisa quieted to my gentle sway.

As I traced the peaceful contours of my daughter's face, I inwardly despaired. A young, first-time mother who knew nothing. I felt bewildered and overwhelmed, confused and incompetent. I wanted to do everything right, to be the best possible mother.

The Christian mamas I knew and looked up to followed the pattern of a well-known book, and with a sinking heart, I resolved to do it their way. But it didn't work for me! I felt like a failure. Neither my baby nor I was thriving under the harsh scheduling the book demanded. I longed to feed her when she was hungry, snuggle her to sleep at my breast, and comfort her every cry. In my heart, I felt the Lord was leading me to nurture her with gentleness and mercy, not with the strict cry-it-out methods the book required. Yet I couldn't let myself follow His leading. Too many voices touted strict scheduling as the right way, and I felt if I couldn't conform, I was somehow doing it wrong.

While I treasured every moment with my infant daughter, that first year was challenging for me emotionally. I didn't follow the book's pattern, not really. I couldn't. But I felt guilty. I felt like my mothering was inferior, and my heart was weighed down by feelings of inadequacy.

For the next two babies, I continued to try and find a balance between following my heart and following the manual. I still struggled, and I still felt embarrassed by my nonconformity as a mama. But somehow, by baby number four, I felt released. I gave up any semblance of trying to schedule my sweet Hope-girl, and I just nurtured her. Bathed in grace and freedom, I nursed her to sleep, carried her in a cloth carrier, and gave myself completely and blissfully to the art of mothering her by heart.

Before I move on, I want to be clear. If the Lord leads you to schedule your sweet ones, and if that method brings peace, stability, and joy to your home, then, please, follow the manual! But don't be tied to that method as the only means of parenting a baby in a Christian home. The point is, when God's Word is not directly instructive, we have freedom in Christ to follow His leading and to be true to the way He has knit our hearts as individuals. My heart was not knit to adhere to a strict feeding schedule for my babies, and I don't think any of my little ones were knit to conform to one either!

Parenting tends to invoke strong opinions about many different issues. As our precious babies grow, the issues grow, too. How do we discipline? How do we educate?

We wrestle beneath our fear of man, because we all want to do it right (oh, and we also want others to notice we've done it right!). We have deep heart desires to see our children grow strong in body, sterling in character, brilliant in mind, steadfast in faith, and successful in all endeavors. We want to be passionate parents who honor Christ, raising passionate kiddos who also honor Christ.

The Bible certainly doesn't leave us flailing in the unknowns of parenting. We are admonished to train our children up in the ways of the Lord. We are commanded to teach them from God's Word, and to love them, to refrain from exasperating them by our inconsistency or hypocrisy, and to, above all, show them the brilliant, beautiful, dazzling gospel-love of Jesus Christ.

Within that framework, there is freedom to wiggle and move and breathe, though. We get to trust God as we walk by faith, individuals parenting individuals.

Spanking, schooling, dating and dress are some of the issues raised in Christian parenting, issues that often come attached with particular expectations for serious-minded believers. It's tough to navigate those decisions under the stifling umbrella of pleasing others. But when we fear God alone, we can wrestle prayerfully with each decision, entrusting our children to their creator and following the Holy Spirit to make decisions that best display the beauty of the gospel within our unique families.

Recently, after three years of homeschooling my girls, my husband and I were presented with a new and enticing option for a private school education. Oh, how we labored over that decision! For months I prayed, asking the Lord to clear the cobwebs of my muddled thinking and give us an answer. Even within my own heart, the decision seemed unclear, but I muddied it so much more by fearing the opinions of others. I would picture a sweet homeschooling mother I wanted to emulate, and I would feel swayed in that direction. Then I would remember that non-believers in the community might more readily accept our family if we chose a more traditional schooling method for our girls. Back and forth. What would this person think? How might so-and-so react? Would I lose friendships or respect one way or another? Often, in my times of prayer, I begged God to remove those chaotic thoughts from my brain so I could dwell in His peace and listen only to His voice. The decision was not a biblical one. It was a matter of our family's preference, and of God's leading. What was His unique calling on our family in the area of education? How could we best shine for His glory as a family? I made the decision so much harder in my incessant man-fearing.

In Christianity, of course, such decision-making freedom is not limited to parenting! We have God-given freedom in how we eat, where we live, to whom and how much we tithe, how we recreate, how we celebrate holidays and special occasions, what music we listen to, and how we dress. We don't have to follow the crowd (even the Christian crowd) on every decision. We can read our Bibles, pray, and trust God to lead us in a gentle dance of grace on the grandstand of our daily lives.

Or, we can cower in fear over in the corner, wondering whether we will ever measure up, whether we will ever get it right.

Proverbs 3: 5-6 says, "Trust in the Lord with all your heart and do not lean on your own understanding. In all your ways acknowledge Him and He will make straight your paths."

I picture a wild meadow of tall, waving grass, dappled with yellow and purple wild flowers. A swampy area cascades into a marshy pond to our right, and on the left a sheer cliff ascends to blue sky like a graceful gray minaret. It is beautiful, but not easy to navigate. And there is our God, not shoveling out a clear, wide trail that stretches clear and easy over the horizon, but pulling a rope to mark our way. As we look to Him, He tugs the rope tight, and makes a straight, taut path through the wild terrain. Our path, our way, is made straight by His hand. He shows us which thorny plants to avoid, which sand-traps to sidestep, which sturdy rocks to step on.

Every believer is drawn only by God and saved only by His grace. In sketching a picture of God's carving a different path for each of us to follow in our earthly lives, please note that the cross is always the starting point. And the gate to the cross, to new life in Christ, is narrow. One way, through the death and resurrection of Jesus.

But our life paths ... well, those aren't all identical. It's not a gravel road clearly marked with wooden signs telling us how to navigate our daily lives. It takes fixing our eyes on Christ for us to see the trail He's straightening out in front of us. If we get pulled down by those weighty old backpacks of man-fearing, we might get lost in the grassy meadow and miss out on God's best. The God who created quaking aspens and fields of arrowleaf balsam root is surely creative enough to design a straight and wondrous path for each of His children.

During the Israelites' desert wanderings, the Lord instructed Moses to send out spies, one from each tribe, in order to give a report of the land they had been promised. Twelve men were appointed and sent, with careful instructions to discern the answers to specific questions. What was the land like? Were the people who lived there strong or weak? Were the cities open or fortified? Were there trees? What sort of fruit did the land bear? The men went up and cautiously spied out the Promised Land. When they returned, they presented their report in front of Moses, Aaron, and all of the people.

The men carried clusters of grapes, pomegranates, and figs into the assembly, displaying the bounty of the fertile land. They said to the people, "We came to the land to which you sent us. It flows with milk and honey, and this is its fruit. However, the people who dwell in the land are strong, and the cities are fortified and very large. And besides, we saw the descendants of Anak there" (Numbers 13:27-28).

The congregation of Israelites began to murmur in concern, and Caleb, the representative of the tribe of Judah, quieted them, saying, "Let us go up at once and occupy it, for we are well able to overcome it" (Numbers 13:30).

The other men argued with Caleb, declaring that the people of the land were too strong, and that the land would devour them.

After hearing their nay-saying, the Israelites rose up in bitter complaint, begging to return to Egypt rather than face the sword of the Canaanites.

Moses and Aaron fell to their faces, overcome with grief and disappointment in their faithless nation. Didn't they trust God after all He had done for them? Caleb and Joshua rent their clothes, passionately beseeching the Israelites to listen. They pleaded, "The land, which we passed through to spy it out, is an exceedingly good land. If the Lord delights in us, he will bring us into this land and give it to us, a land that flows with milk and honey. Only do not rebel against the Lord and do not fear the people of the land, for they are bread for us. Their protection is removed from them, and the Lord is with us; do not fear them" (Numbers 14:7-10).

Instead of heeding their impassioned plea, the Israelites wanted to stone Joshua and Caleb. But in the midst of the riot, the glory of the Lord appeared, shining radiant and angry in the meeting tent. God wanted to smite His fearful, disloyal, and faithless people. Moses begged the Lord to preserve His own powerful reputation by sparing the Israelites and to pardon their iniquity because of His great lovingkindness. The Lord forgave the Israelites as Moses asked, but their grave unbelief did not go without consequences.

For forty years, the Israelites would remain nomads in the desert, suffering for their unfaithfulness. No man over the age of twenty would be permitted to enter the Promised Land; they would die in the desert. Only the children of God's chosen people would live to glimpse the beauty God had prepared for them. Because of their grumbling and their disbelief, they would not see God's reward. Only their offspring would pluck grapes and figs from the trees of the Promised Land and witness God's power over the land's seemingly impenetrable fortresses.

The children … and Joshua and Caleb. The two men who had spoken brave and faithful words of encouragement to God's people would also be allowed to enter. They had seen the fearsome obstacles standing in their way, but, unlike the other ten spies, they had seen them in light of God's mighty strength. They had known God would go before them, and they were unafraid. They had anticipated the outstretched hand of God clearing a path for them into the land, overtaking their enemies, and toppling their walled cities. They had feared God. "Do not rebel against God, and do not fear the people!" they had shouted at the frightened Israelite mob.

The ten spies—the ten cowering, scared spies—had sacrificed God's reward because of their fear of man. They didn't believe God was big enough to handle the challenges ahead and their disbelief cost them greatly.

Caleb and Joshua, on the other hand, trusted God. They believed His promises, were convinced of His goodness, and knew He was mightier than any earthly power. And they received His reward when they watched Jericho crumble and tasted the sweetness of the Promised Land.

When we fear man, we miss out on God's greater reward.

Let's be like Caleb and Joshua. Let's throw off the fear of man that ensnares us, and follow the admonition of Hebrews 12:1-2, which says, "Therefore, since we are surrounded by so great a cloud of witnesses, let us also lay aside every weight, and sin which clings so closely, and let us run with endurance the race that is set before us, looking to Jesus, the founder and perfecter of our faith, who for the joy set before Him endured the cross, despising the shame, and is seated at the right hand of the throne of God."

CHAPTER FOUR:
A Rose by Any Other Name

Sometimes, in order to move past the sin that hinders us in our walks with God, we have to call it by its name. A rose by any other name might still smell as sweet, but calling sin by any other name allows us to minimize it. Sugar coating sin with worldly terminology lessens its seriousness in our eyes. If we think our sin is merely an "issue," we risk fighting it with the wrong weapons. To do battle with sin—with the power of the Holy Spirit and the tools of God's Word—we have to call it sin.

We have to move past calling our fear of man a struggle, tendency, or personality quirk, and we have to call it what it is. Sin against God. A fear of man that upstages the fear we are *supposed* to have for our awesome God.

As a nineteen-year-old college junior, I decided to go out for the cross-country team at my small (Division III) university. I had participated in track and field the previous two years, as a sprinter and jumper. But a semester abroad had awakened a new enjoyment of distance running, and I decided to see if there was anything competitive in my slow-twitch muscles.

It turned out that there was. As I trained and raced, I discovered my aptitude for endurance running was far greater than my aptitude for the short events. I was a much better distance runner than I was a sprinter, and I achieved greater success that season than I ever expected. But, somewhere in between an uphill 5K and a grueling interval workout, my internal perfectionism reared its ugly head. I decided that I needed to conform to the "right" prototype for female cross-county runners. I was too tall, for one thing. I couldn't change that, but I was also a good twenty pounds heavier than the other leading runners on our team. So I decided to concentrate my efforts there. Slowly, I moderated my eating choices, depriving my body of the food it needed so my frame and weight would conform to the standard I thought was expected of me. By the following summer, I had lost nearly forty pounds. Unfortunately, I was weak, tired, and struggled to run or even jog. Late in the summer, I realized that restricting my diet had become the consuming drive of my day-to-day life. I was no longer just controlling what I ate. Now, what I ate was controlling me.

I reached out for help and entered a counseling program for eating disorder recovery. I had a wonderfully kind and gentle Christian counselor who asked me probing questions about my past, about wounds and scars and buried feelings. I am sure her kind encouragement and weekly account-ability propelled me forward in recovery. Her gentle care of me is actually a fond memory. But, I did not turn around and choose healthy eating patterns because of psychology.

Rather, as I opened my heart to God, and told Him I was so entangled in this mess of unhealthy choices, He showed me that my drastic self-focus was a sin against Him. It wasn't just a psychological disorder; it was a pattern of sin and selfishness. It was the fear of man, trapping me in a web of wrong thinking. I was wrapped up in myself, instead of being wrapped up in God. I had traded the truth that my frail human body was a mere vessel for God to use for the lie that my body shape and size were all that mattered. We are to care for our bodies as God's temples—not abuse them for the sake of a worldly beauty standard.

So I confessed that my eating disorder was truly a sin against my cre-ator. I asked for His help to view my body correctly, biblically. And I began to eat.

In my own story, an eating disorder was one manifestation of a larger problem—a desire to be perfect in my own strength, to please others, and to be seen or thought of in a certain way.

Let's say my fear of man grew to be such a consuming force that I became paralyzed in social settings. Perhaps I would visit a counselor, and I would hear that I needed to develop self-confidence, that I needed to love myself and learn to be comfortable with who I was. Those things might be true to some extent, but they would also be deeply flawed strategies for real healing. They would miss the point. They would direct me back to my own flawed heart—to my sinful preoccupation with myself.

Just as I needed to confess that my eating disorder was sin, I also need to confess that my overwhelming concern with human opinion is also a sin. I am a glory-stealer. I want others to see and give me glory when I should be pointing them to the awesome glory of our God.

It's not just a personality trait. It's an offense against my creator. It is, essentially, idolatry.

In Exodus 20:3, the Lord commands His people, "You shall have no other gods before me." Maybe we don't have bright prayer flags waving in front of our homes, and maybe we don't bow down before life-size statues of Buddha, or burn incense in our homes as we pray to our personal shrines.

But in our hearts, we fail to worship God alone.

Here is what God actually commands of us—what He really means when He says we shall have no other gods before Him, "And he said to him, 'You shall love the Lord your God with all your heart and with all your soul and with all your mind. This is the first and greatest commandment'" (Matthew 22:37-38).

Elyse Fitzpatrick elaborates on this passage in her book, *Idols of the Heart*:

What is our Lord commanding here? Nothing less than our undivided love and worship. Just as soon as I pause to reflect on that principal command, I begin to get uncomfortable. I have to ask myself,

- *Do I love Him with everything that I am, or are there other loves in my heart that clamor for my attention?*

- *Do I worship additional gods, or is He always, and in every case, the supreme Ruler who receives my undivided passion and devotion?*[15]

Idolatry is not just the worship of a false god in a purely religious sense. Idolatry has to do with our love. What do we love? If we do not love Jesus above all else, then we are idolators. Our hearts are tainted with the wrong priorities of love gone awry. We don't have room in our hearts for undefiled worship of our creator because a bigger love of self and the world have overtaken our heart's gardens with thorny weeds. When I was caught in the trap of anorexia, the love of being thin and beautiful was like a strangling idol-weed in my heart.

The approval of man can become an idol in our hearts. When we love the applause of God's people more than we desire the fame and glory of God Himself, that's idolatry. When we fear man instead of bowing down before God alone, that's idolatry.

It is sin.

I wanted to set the record straight at the outset of this chapter. Let's call sin, sin so we can demolish its stronghold in our lives through the power of the Holy Spirit. The world would have very different strategies for helping you and me shed our preoccupation with others' approval, and the way they would have us do it is not biblical. To see ourselves, others, and God through a lens of biblical truth, we have to confess our sin—not just acknowledge our self-consciousness as a thread of our personalities.

To keep this from sounding overly harsh, will you get up from wherever you are sitting and brew yourself something warm and comforting? Grab a mug of your favorite latte or herbal tea and curl your knees up to your chest as you nestle into a cozy chair. I will steep some dark Assam tea in my favorite cracked teapot and join you.

Are you settled in? I am not wagging a condemning finger. I promise. As I sort this out in my own sin-tangled heart, I long to come along side you, and help you, too, to unearth places in your life where a wrong perspective of God and man has hindered you from living fully.

There is idolatry inherent in our fear of man. It is not sinful that we desire relationships with people. It is not even sinful to want to be liked, or to desire a solid, respectable reputation. But we have seen in previous chapters how those desires become inordinate and consuming.

Elyse Fitzpatrick says, "Remember that your strongest desires, the things that you are most passionate about, are what ultimately define your worship. If you passionately desire the respect of others, then your life will be colored by the fear of man. You'll worship other people's opinions. If you intensely crave acceptance, you'll be terrified of loneliness and rejection. You'll serve gods of man pleasing, peer pressure, or codependency." [16]

Can you see how that is true? It is painful to let that truth settle over our hearts. I don't want to admit that I love my Lord less than I love the opinions of people! I don't want to confess that I have served other gods. But I have. Tears well in my eyes as I type those words, because I don't want to bow before the idol of man pleasing. I know God alone deserves my worship, and I am so very grateful He forgives me when I fail to give Him all of it! He is so gracious with us as we fumble with our lesser gods—not willing that we should continue in our sin, but, oh, so willing to restore us!

Dr. Edward Welch likens people to "love tanks with a leak,"[17] all of us wandering around seeking the love and approval of other people to meet our needs and fill our emptiness. We are yawning, wide open cups, slanted upward to await the love-filling. But we are cracked and broken and we leak, and the pitchers that pour liquid love in can never quite fill us.

One of the key factors leading us to pick up the backpack of man-fearing is that we feel needs that are not legitimate. We look to the world around us to have our emotional needs met, to fill us. We imagine deep psychological needs, needs we feel must be met if we are to experience happiness, fullness. And then we look to other people to fill our needs, to meet our desires. Because we put the burden of our happiness on others' ability to meet our needs, we become codependent, man-fearing glory-thieves.

Not only do we look to have our needs met in the wrong places, we also have the wrong needs to begin with! We have needs and desires that put us and our happiness at the forefront. Rather, God and His glory should be the centerpiece of our lives.

The truth is, what we perceive as needs are not needs at all. They are desires, blown out of proportion and looming dangerously large in our lives.

I do not need the admiration and respect of my coworkers. I do not need the most well-kept, lovely home in the neighborhood. I do not need a body that is in peak, competitive fitness shape all of the time. I do not need fashionable clothes straight off the runway. I do not need perfect, well-behaved children I can be self-righteously proud of. I do not need a husband who appreciates all the little things I do to serve him and who serves me in return. I do not need a fancy car, or a sparkling diamond ring. I do not need to be known, to be noticed, or to be thought well of.

I may have longings, wants, and lusts. But my needs, my real, spiritual, God-given needs, are all met in Jesus at the cross, and through His people as we together seek to accomplish His purposes.

Let's clarify that thought a little further. Take a long drink of your hot tea. Together, let's wrap our hands around our warm mugs and our minds around these complex truths.

Human beings are not self-sustaining creatures. We have physical needs that must be met in order for us to survive. We need sustenance, shelter, water. We can't live without them.

We are spiritually bankrupt, bereft and empty. We need Christ to redeem us from bondage to sin, to set us free, to give us life. We need Him to fill our emptiness with His great love and to pour out His equipping, purpose-giving *charis* grace on our lives. We need Jesus.

And we need the body of Christ, rounding out our individual deficiencies and limitations in order to present the fullness of Christ and His glory to the world around us. Ephesians 4:15-16 says, "Rather, speaking the truth in love, we are to grow up in every way into him who is the head, into Christ, from whom the whole body, joined and held together by every joint with which it is equipped, when each part is working properly, makes the body grow so that it builds itself up in love."

We don't need each other to bolster our self-esteem, to flatter each other, or to meet our emotional lusts for approval. We need each other to fulfill the purposes Christ has designed for His church. We need the arms, the legs, and the eyes of the church body to function in unity so God can be glorified and proclaimed in us together. I can't teach or lead the way my talented husband does. And I don't have the organizational skills of our wonderful children's ministry director. I can't dissect Greek grammar like my deep-thinking pastor, and I am not a bold evangelist like my beautiful, red-haired sister-in-law. But I am a mercy-giver, a nurturer, and a haven-maker. And I am needed, too. So are you, with whatever spiritual gifts God has crafted in you!

To move past our sinful reliance on man's opinion, to be released from that controlling fear, we have to abandon our pursuit of illegitimate needs and focus on the real needs God has fashioned in our bodies and our spirits.[18]

Let's go back to the imaginary psychologist's office and sit down on the edge of her leather sofa. She has an answer for our codependent, self-conscious lack of confidence. It's the answer the world gives; it's the answer our culture (and sometimes even the church) perpetuates.

We need to esteem ourselves. We need to love ourselves, accept ourselves, and embrace the quirks and characteristics that make us who we are. We need to stop worrying about what other people think and be confident in our own inner beauty.

Right? We just need to look inward, discover our unique value, and move forward with grace and confidence because of the beauty inherent in our souls. It is only our self-doubt that keeps us from inhabiting our own loveliness with poise and charm.

It sounds lovely, doesn't it? Grow a little self-esteem. Love yourself. Sweep away the fear of man as you let your true and alluring self shimmer bravely and beautifully in fresh inner confidence. Dwell comfortably in your own skin and walk with your head held high.

It sounds lovely, yes. But it's not true. Or biblical. It's not accurate to describe humans as beings imbued with inner beauty that is merely stifled by fear and doubt.

Self-esteem is a bit of a modern fallacy.

If that statement ruffles your feathers a little bit, please hang in there with me. In order to fully explain what I mean by "self-esteem is a fallacy," we need to back up a little. In fact, we need to back up all the way to the dawn of time, when God created humankind in His image. Genesis 1:27 says, "So

God created man in his image, in the image of God he created him; male and female he created them."

At creation, God sculpted man in His own likeness, a living creature to embody the goodness of God. Man had reason, intelligence, and emotions. And at that moment, in the whole, blissfully unbroken garden, man was without sin. Adam and Eve were good, as God was good. They were beautiful because God had given them His beauty.

But the fall—the deceit of the serpent, the disobedience of God's beloved, and the destruction of all that was perfect and undefiled in the world—forever altered any inherent goodness in us. Scripture tells us that each baby who bursts forth from his mother's womb, naked, squalling, and covered in fluid and blood, is born, not into innocent beauty, but into sin.

Romans 5:12 tells us, "Therefore, just as sin came into the world through one man, and death through sin, and so death spread to all men because all sinned …"

And Romans 3:10-12 reminds us, "None is righteous, no, not one; no one understands; no one seeks for God. All have turned aside; together they have become worthless; no one does good, not even one."

Our hearts are not intrinsically beautiful. We are defiled by sin, naked, and needy. God reaches out in His perfect love and rescues us from the shame of our sin. "While we were sinners, Christ died for us!" Romans 5:8 declares.

It is not until we receive the gift of salvation, exchange the ugliness of our sin-stained hearts for hearts reborn in Jesus, that we can possess any true beauty or goodness. Anything good or worthy in us is Christ alone!

"Do we have value to God even before we are redeemed?" author Leslie Ludy asks in her book *Set-Apart Femininity:*

> *Yes! God does love us and see us as valuable before we are redeemed, but it is not because we are attractive to Him and it's not because we possess anything worthwhile,*

inwardly or outwardly. It is because He Himself is Love personified, and He longs to rescue us from our ugly, reviled state and place His divine, Heavenly beauty upon us. The great preacher Charles Spurgeon said it perfectly: "If a soul has any beauty, it is because Christ has endowed that soul with His own, for in ourselves we are deformed and defiled! There is no beauty in any of us but what our Lord has worked in us.[19]

If there is beauty in us—it is the beauty of Christ. His perfect, sinless life was broken and poured out at the cross, so He could showcase His glory through the redemption of His people. He uses each of us differently, to be sure, and we each reflect His glory through the mold and shape of our own God-given personalities. Yet, it is never *our* beauty that should be glorified. Overcoming insecurity is not about embracing the uniqueness of our inner lives; it is about laying down our concern with self, and embracing the wonder, the power, and the perfect beauty of Jesus Christ.[20]

Here is where the false idea of self-esteem comes in. We are not meant to esteem ourselves! We are called to humility. Philippians 2:3-4 tells us, "Do nothing from rivalry or conceit, but in humility count others more significant than yourselves. Let each of you look not only to his own interests but also to the interests of others."

We are not supposed to coddle flesh and be comfortable with who we are. Rather, "those who belong to Christ have crucified the flesh with its passions and desires" (Galatians 5:24). We are supposed to annihilate our fleshly passions and live by the Spirit.

Romans 12:3 adds, "For by the grace given to me I say to everyone among you not to think of himself more highly than he ought to think, but to think with sober judgment, each according to the measure of faith that God has assigned."

You might interpret sober thinking to include a measure of self-esteem in that verse. After all, we are told not to think *too* highly of ourselves, but a right view of ourselves might include a bit of healthy self love, right? And the command to "love your neighbor as yourself," assumes that we need to love ourselves first, doesn't it?

Here is the thing, though. The Bible never assumes that we need to work on loving ourselves. It is natural in our sinful nature to think mostly, primarily, and consuming-ly about our own interests. We don't need to love ourselves so we can love our neighbor; we need to crucify our selfishness so we can love others the way we already, naturally, and often sinfully care deeply about our own needs.

Even someone with a seemingly low view of herself, someone who is shy and backwards and lost because she has such a low self-confidence, is really just preoccupied with self. If I think constantly about how much worse I am than everyone around me, if I fixate on how I can never measure up, I am still trapped in a dreary cave of self-focus.

We don't need self-esteem. We need to lay down self and esteem God highly. We need to obliterate our preoccupation with ourselves and become consumed with making much of God.

A set-apart believer with a right fear of our holy God will not be consumed with thoughts of how the world views her. Rather, she (or he) will be utterly focused on how God can be glorified and made known through her.

John 1:1-4 says, "In the beginning was the Word, and the Word was with God, and the Word was God. He was in the beginning with God. All things were made through him and without him was not anything made that was made. In him was life, and the life was the light of men."

In the beginning was God: Father, Son, and Holy Spirit. In a perfectly balanced partnership they breathed life and wonder into the formless void. This world, this story, starts with God, ends with God, and is all about God.

He is the central character in the grand romance unfolding on the universe's stage. He is the author, the principal actor, the director. He has, miraculously and kindly, set His affections on us—His created people. But we are not the stars of the world's play. He is!

And that is why self-esteem is a fallacy.

In the book of Genesis, we read many stories about the patriarchs of Israel, the founding fathers of the Jewish nation. The lineage is familiar. Abraham fathered Isaac, whose wife Rebekah bore twin sons, Esau and Jacob. When the time came for Jacob to marry, Isaac sent him on a pilgrimage to Rebekah's brother's family. The house of Laban received Jacob with joy, and Jacob began to work for his uncle. After a month's time had passed, Laban approached Jacob to ask what he would like to receive as wages for his labor.

Laban had two daughters. Leah was the oldest, and the Bible tells us her "eyes were weak" (Genesis 29:17). While Rachel was lovely in form and appearance, Leah was plain, with pale-colored eyes that seemed to fade and dim when contrasted with Rachel's sparkling, deep-colored ones. Although Leah was older, she hid, dowdy and unappreciated, behind the glowing radiance of her younger sister.

And Jacob loved Rachel. So, when Laban asked Jacob what he would like to receive as compensation for his work, Jacob asked for Rachel. For seven years, Jacob served Laban, waiting for the day when Rachel would become his wife. Finally, the day arrived. Laban prepared a wedding feast and Jacob celebrated his good fortune with all of the gathered guests. Evening fell, and Jacob became one with his bride. Perhaps robes hid his new wife's face from him in the darkness; perhaps the evening's libations had dulled his senses. Jacob believed he had gone to bed with Rachel, but, somehow, "in the morning, behold, it was Leah!" (verse 25).

Laban insisted that the customs of their country required the older daughter to be married first. He offered Rachel to Jacob as a second wife, in exchange for another seven years of labor. Jacob agreed.

Meanwhile, the Lord looked compassionately on Leah. He saw that she was unloved. Jacob fulfilled his duties by Leah, but he hated her. He rejected her. And Leah? She idolized Jacob. She longed for his love and affection. She ached to be beautiful in his eyes.

God opened Leah's womb and she conceived a son. She called him Reuben, and said, "Because the Lord has looked upon my affliction; for now my husband will love me" (verse 32). She conceived again, and bore a second son, Simeon. "Because the Lord has heard that I am hated, He has given me this son also" she said (verse 33). Her third son was Levi, and Leah said, "Now this time my husband will be attached to me, because I have borne him three sons" (verse 34).

Can you hear Leah's desperation? Oh, how she longed for Jacob's approval. As she held her newborn babies, nurtured them at her breast, and carried them with her as she went about her day's work, she ached for Jacob to notice her. To see her sons and take pride in them—in her! She yearned for him to treat her with the affection of a husband to a beloved wife. Her fear of Jacob was her idol.

Leah conceived again. At some point during this pregnancy and birth, Leah let go of her idolatry. She basked in the Lord's lovingkindness. God cared deeply about her plight and intervened repeatedly on her behalf. The Bible doesn't tell us what shifted in Leah's spirit, or how the Lord touched and changed her. But something happened. She began to worship God alone. Before, she had prayed in desperation for God to help her, but it was Jacob whose approval she worshiped. When her fourth son was born, Leah proclaimed, "This time I will praise the Lord" (verse 36). She named him Judah.

Leah went on to have two more sons and a daughter, but Judah was chosen by God in a special way. Is it merely coincidence that Judah is the tribe from which the Messiah came? When Leah fixed her eyes on God, praising Him for His goodness, regardless of whether Jacob loved her, Judah was born. The child born into praise was the child whose line would include King David, and ultimately Jesus. When Leah worshiped God and feared Him alone, God could use her for His Kingdom purposes.

CHAPTER FIVE:
Mingling Love and Fear

Theologians separate the Word of God into categories in several ways. First, of course, are the Testaments, the Old and the New. The Old Testament spans the history of God and man up until four-hundred years before the birth of Jesus. The New Testament picks up at the "fullness of time" after the four-hundred years of silence have ended and the Messiah is nestled waiting in the womb of a young Jewish girl named Mary.

We categorize further by groupings of books: the history books, the books of poetry, the prophets (both major and minor), the gospels, and the epistles. There are sixty-six books that make up the Bible, named sometimes after their content or subject, sometimes for their author, and sometimes for the recipient of the letter.

Some Bible scholars also divide the Bible into dispensations. There are usually thought to be seven or eight dispensations, although some theologians simplify those eight into three or four. A dispensation is a period of time where God dealt with His people in a particular way, based upon how much of His redemption plan had already been revealed to them. Salvation has always come through faith in Christ, but those born under the Old Covenant—the Old Testament believers—trusted in God for a Messiah who had not yet come. They believed God and trusted Him for salvation with as much information and revelation as they had already received. They did not know the full story.

It is not a perfect parallel, but, as I look back over my own faith journey and my own limited (but growing) understanding of God and His ways, I think my personal life has its own groupings, its own categories. Not quite dispensations, but segments of life where my relationship with the Lord looked a certain way, and then changed.

Can you trace your walk of faith that way, too? Can you remember Sunday school lessons or Christmas pageants, childish hymns with poignant theology, flannel boards and puppet shows? For me, a vague understanding of God formed, wispy and fluttering, as I flounced along to weekly catechism class in frilly dresses, listened to canticles and hymns in an ornate sanctuary, and walked a long hall to a brick-walled Sunday school room where I heard simple Bible stories about Jesus. Maybe you missed that innocent, early dispensation. Maybe your first picture of God was drawn in the bright, neon colors of a church youth group, where music blared with a heady drum beat and the gospel came peppered with the words "dude" and "cool." My teen years brought a clearer picture of God, as I scratched the surface of truth with Wednesday morning prayer breakfasts, Friday night devotionals, and frequent drop-ins to my youth pastor's office. I listened to speakers teach about creationism and evangelism and other isms at weekend conferences, and I scribbled notes during Sunday sermons. The misty picture became a bit more bold and defined, but the middle, the heart, was still uncolored.

I attended a Christian university, where, unfortunately, the Bible department wavered in its position on things like the inerrancy of Scripture, and a literal interpretation of Genesis. The edges of my bold understanding began to dim on that beautiful campus of rose gardens, historic buildings, and postmodern doubt. So, I decided to head to Bible college in Austria for a semester, hoping to sharpen my Bible knowledge and grow in wisdom so I could intelligently battle apologetics with the wishy-washy professors back at university.

Instead, I learned that knowledge meant nothing without relationship. I could know *about* God, or I could know God Himself, worshipping Him in spirit and in truth. God longs for relationship; the Bible teaches us He woos His children, tenderly pursuing them with His gift of mercy and the offer to become a part of His eternal Bride. In Austria, I jogged up alpine trails, praying and listening, mesmerized by blue skies, snow-bonneted Alps, and the clang of distant cowbells. I meandered mountain villages with my heart open and my hands lifted high, calling out to God, who seemed nearer and somehow more touchable than He ever had. I sipped tea with kindred spirits, and prayed with them—that we would know God and love Him. I studied Scripture, yes, but I did so with a heart that sought relationship with my creator, rather than just head knowledge of who He is.

In my post-college years and as a young wife, I studied the Christian disciplines and experimented with new ways of experiencing and worshipping God. I centered my quiet times with scripted, repetitive prayers that focused my mind on the pursuit of dwelling in Christ. I partook of the Lord's Supper in the quiet of my own kitchen, dunking chunks of crusty bread in glasses of grape juice to taste and remember His sacrifice. I still studied my Bible daily (or at least almost daily), but I also explored new disciplines of the Christian faith in order to expand my understanding of worship.

As a new mama, I held my baby girl and knew that my deepest desire for my child was that she would know God and love Him deeply. I prayed that He would save her, that she would follow Him, that she would live her life passionately in service to Him. And, as I prayed, my own walk with the Lord changed. It wasn't just about me knowing God; it was about how I could impart a knowledge and love of God to my children. I began to think in child-like terms about everything I knew of theology.

Why, you might wonder, am I sharing the phases of my personal Christian walk with you? Here is the thing. Our understanding and our experience of God change over time. We understand Him dimly, in basic terms and definitions, and we grow. Our styles of worship shift; our Bible study methods evolve to suit our personalities and our stages of life. But God does not change. He is immutable. He is not altered by the shifting shadows or the crumbling foundations of mortality in our culture. The God I have only begun to understand and know is the same, yesterday, today, and forever. He is always holy, always just, always loving, and always worthy of our utmost worship. While you and I may find that we experience God or worship Him in different fashions, our God is one and the same—so long as we are worshipping the true God of the Bible.

My husband is a naturalist. While I feel closest to God while sitting at my shabby-chic (more shabby than chic) dining table, reading, praying and journaling in the early morning, my spirit quieted with a cup of steaming tea and a flickering vanilla-scented candle, Erik draws near to God by exploring His creation. When he hikes a wilderness trail or paddles a canoe across a lake at sunrise—the sky tinged pink and the world around him hushed—he worships the Lord. He experiences the beauty of God in the outdoors.

Our pathways look different. Our styles of worship look different. Our pursuit of God through spiritual disciplines looks different. But God is God. And any true worship, any right worship, begins at the same place.

True worship, and true freedom in Christ, begin with a right fear of God.

We've talked a lot about the ways we exchange a "big" view of God for a larger-than-life perspective of people. We fear people, not God, and as we trudge on, burdened by the weight of all that misplaced fear, we can't see His full glory. He seems insignificant to us, because we have made people too important, too weighty. In order for us to shed the heavy packs stuffed with our mess of man-fearing, we have to develop a proper fear of the Lord. We have to see His greatness and bow down before it. So, let's start by examining who God is—how great and perfect and utterly beautiful is the King of glory.

When my husband bows in humble awe at the sight of a bald eagle swooping down over the river, or when he marvels at tiny black bear cubs tumbling clumsy down a tree trunk, or laughs giddy at lightning streaking through rain-washed sky, He is praising God as creator. That's a good place to start.

The Message (a Bible paraphrase) offers lyrical interpretations of the Psalms. Listen to this sing-song praise to God, the author and sustainer of life, found in Psalm 104:

> O my soul, bless God! God, my God, how great you are! Beautifully, gloriously robed, dressed up in sunshine, and all heaven stretched out for your tent. You built your palace on the ocean deeps, made a chariot out of clouds and took off on wind-wings. You commandeered winds as messengers, appointed fire and flame as ambassadors. You set earth on a firm foundation so that nothing can shake it, ever. You blanketed earth with ocean, covered the mountains with deep waters; then you roared and the water ran away—your thunder crash put it to flight. Mountains pushed up, valleys spread out in the places you assigned them. You set boundaries between earth and sea; never again will earth be flooded. You started the springs and rivers, sent them flowing among the hills ... You water the mountains from your heavenly cisterns ...
>
> What a wildly wonderful world, God! You made it all, with Wisdom at your side, made earth overflow with your wonderful creations. Oh, look—the deep, wide sea, brimming with fish past counting ... All the creatures look expectantly to you to give them their meals on time. You come, and they gather around; you open your hand and they eat from it. If you turned your back, they'd die in a minute—take back your Spirit and they die, revert to

original mud; send out your Spirit and they spring to life—
the whole countryside in bloom and blossom.

The glory of God—let it last forever! Let God enjoy
His creation (Psalm 104, MSG).

The first reason to fear God is that He is our maker. Did you catch some of that imagery? God, garbed in radiance, stretched out the heavens, unrolled the firmament, poured out the deep, and clashed tectonic plates together so mountains would protrude in jagged splendor. The winds heed His whisper; they trot to and fro at His bidding. Remember the storm on the Sea of Galilee? The scared disciples? And, the wild wind that recognized the voice of Jesus as the very voice whose whispered breath became the first breeze. "Be still," he said, and the wind obeyed.

Here's another nugget from Psalms, chapter 68, "Sing, O kings of the earth! Sing praises to the Lord! There he is: Sky Rider, striding the ancient skies. Listen—he's calling in thunder, rumbling, rolling thunder. Call out 'Bravo' to God, the High God of Israel. His splendor and strength rise huge as thunderheads" (MSG).

At the table, I hold a lump of clay in my hands, roll it, twist it, wind it through my fingers. What can I make from this ball of shapeless dough? I try to craft something simple—a little pony to prance across my table and make my almost two-year-old giggle. My horse has fat legs. His muzzle is pointy where it should be rounded. Its mane is just three thin ropes of clay dangling limply down a neck that is too long. A giraffe maybe? I am not particularly artistic, obviously, but Hope laughs as the little trotter heads recklessly towards her.

I can't even make a recognizable horse out of modeling clay. But, God? He shaped the world! He flung stars into the galaxy, millions of them. He made them glimmer with heat so that our earthly nights would sparkle beneath a canopy of diamonds. He made animals—from tiny one-celled organisms to amazingly complex sea creatures and massive elephants that thunder across dusty plains. He molded humans from dust. He created every system of our bodies to work just so—and we can breathe, walk, digest food, speak, learn, create, and birth new life. Our every heartbeat is a miracle of His creation.

We live in the valley of the Tetons, here in Wyoming. Every day, I look out my window, and if the sky is clear, I can see the peaks soaring white and rugged. They are full of His majesty. There is a fault line that tells the geologic story of their creation, but I know the deeper truth. God assigns the boundaries of the mountains, and they shout loud of His magnificence. Trumpeter swans sound their call as they fly over my house in the spring, and I watch their wings spread wide. A moose nibbles willows in my yard when the snow is deep, and I chuckle because these strong and feisty animals are so gangly, so funny-looking, with their long legs and comical faces. In mid-summer, mountain thunderstorms rattle our house, shaking tree branches ruthlessly into the backyard and pelting hail that ripples the pond. Shafts of blinding white light split the sky from top to bottom.

Romans 1:20 says, "For his invisible attributes, namely, his eternal power and divine nature, have been clearly perceived, ever since the creation of the world, in the things that were made. So they are without excuse."

The created world demonstrates God's power and creativity, and when we see all that He has made, we should be in awe of Him! My little clay horse is small, pitiful, and lifeless. God created life and beauty that boggles the mind and stirs the heart. We can't do that.

Psalm 24:1-3 tells us, "The earth is the Lord's and the fullness thereof, the world and those who dwell therein, for he has founded it upon the seas and established it upon the rivers. Who shall ascend the hill of the Lord? And who shall stand in his holy place?"

And in verse 10, the psalmist goes on to say, "Who is this King of glory? The Lord of hosts, he is the King of glory!"

God created every single cell of life on this earth. He molded the shape and form of the universe: the vast oceans and the geysers spouting steam and water into the sky, the jagged mountains and the burbling mud-pots, the flowering trees and the bright rings circling the planet Saturn. All of it is His! God the creator is worthy of our heart's deepest awe.

He created the world, and He holds it together.

Sometimes it feels like His hand slips, doesn't it? We talk about the beauty and the wonder, but there is also a great, trembling, and seemingly chaotic power that tips our world topsy-turvy. There are hurricanes, tornados, earthquakes, and fires. God's "got the whole world in His hands," we sing with our little ones, but is God the creator really God the sovereign? Is the author of life truly also the sustainer of it?

I believe He is. I believe the great hands that hold the globe are gentle, loving, and steady. Sin broke God's creation, right? But sin could not thwart His purposes or His love for His people. He wove a plan, and that plan included man's free will, his choice of whether to follow God. God couldn't undo the disastrous effects of sin on the earth without also severing the freedom of man to choose. Sin had shattered what had once been perfect, and now we had to learn to live in relationship with God while still tangled in the messiness of a sin-scarred world (and the seeping ugliness of our own sin-stained hearts).

God is kind and sovereign, and His strong hands hold us in a protective balance while still allowing sin to wreak its apparent havoc. Do you see how much grace there is on earth? Even for every instance of tragedy and disaster? Do you see God at work, weaving mercy and love into our lives?

My stomach often churns when I read the newspaper. It is summertime now in our bustling, mountain tourist town. Every week, the newspaper chronicles another loss. A climber fell from a staggering height. A woman drowned while on the river. A motorcyclist rear-ended a stopped car. I read and my spirit crumples, because people hurt!

But, hundreds of climbers miraculously held sure and safe on their ropes and crags. Thousands of rafters floated safe through whitewater sections on the Snake River. Countless cars drove safely through busy intersections, in spite of distractions, confusion, and mistakes. We somehow expect those things as a privilege, rather than experiencing safety and beauty as a gift.

God gives so much grace. It's not that He holds the world, and sometimes He lets go for an instant. It's that He holds the world, and sometimes His hands (and His aching Father's heart) allow suffering and destruction to sift through. Sin *did* wreak havoc, but even in all the blustery, storming mess of pain, God protects us, gives us His mercy, and fashions goodness. In ways we don't really understand, God's glory is revealed through all of it.

God is writing our stories. When He allows suffering in our lives, He weaves it into our stories with the colors of His gospel glory. He doesn't watch pain fall, wasted and useless. He transforms us through it, comforts us in the midst of it, stitches something new and even more beautiful from the scraps. He gives us "gold for these ashes."

God, the artist, is creating a masterpiece much larger than what we can see in the space immediately surrounding our own small lives. We see a mishmash of tangled thread, but, from the viewpoint of our creator, our corner of disordered color is just a tiny part of a grand picture. God's great tapestry puts the gospel on display with vibrant brilliance. We just don't see the whole picture.

I don't pretend to comprehend all the intricacies of balancing God's sovereignty with our human freedom, or the daily gifts of God's grace contrasted with the darkness of lives marred by sin. Part of the reason we fear

God is because He is beyond us. His ways don't completely make sense to us, because, well, we're not God!

We don't understand everything God is doing, because God is in a class by Himself. He is holy, set-apart, and utterly different than any created being. The holiness ascribed to God denotes two sets of attributes. The first is the absoluteness of God. He is not a created being. He is Yaweh, the "I AM." Before anything else existed, the triune God reigned in all His perfect majesty. He is powerful, wonderful, and completely amazing. "Holy, Holy, Holy is the Lord of hosts; the whole earth is full of His glory!" it says in Isaiah 6:3. We cannot even begin to grasp all of who God is! The fact that I am attempting to write a chapter explaining aspects of God's character and why He is worthy of our fear is a bit laughable—because our God is so far beyond my frail explanations. My fumbling words chase gossamer threads of beauty that waft through my understanding. Like a butterfly net sweeping empty through the sky, I can't seem to catch the ethereal truth with my simple, small words.

God is also holy in terms of His purity. He is holy in His bold, unique, set-apartness, and He is holy in His sinless character, His separation from anything evil. Sometimes we think of goodness as an absence of evil. But God's pure goodness is so far above our connotations! He is so good that evil is not even a thought in Him. His goodness is just *good*! This is an ethical holiness. It is a purity of heart, a perfection that is shining white in its cleanliness. And God's ethical holiness is the holiness we are told to emulate. Ephesians 1:4 tells believers, "… He chose us in him before the foundation of the world, that we should be holy and blameless before Him." We can't be holy in the first sense of the word, but by God's grace in our lives, we can begin to resemble Him in the purity and righteousness of our lives—both in our outward expressions of faith and the inward motivations of our hearts. We can strive to be holy as God is holy by devoting ourselves to seeking the honor of God.

God's holiness is another reason we fear Him.

The amazing attributes of God summon a deep awe in our hearts, don't they? God is perfect. We are not, and so we ought to bow low, humble, and reverent.

Remember when I mentioned how, as a mama, I rethink all I know of God in terms of how I can share it with my daughters? I digest and metabolize truth in order to regurgitate it for my sweet ones. I love collecting well-written devotional resources to read together—preferably with cups of hot tea all around (have you noticed my affinity for that soothing beverage, yet?). Recently, I stumbled upon a book called *God's Wisdom* by Sally Michael. I was thrilled to discover a few chapters about the fear of God within its pages, so bear with me as I quote a bit from this wonderful children's book.

"Do you stand in awe of God? God is not just 'good at everything He does.' He is more than good. He is perfect in everything He does and all that He is. He is perfect in power, perfect in knowledge, perfect in love, perfect in beauty, perfect in justice, perfect in mercy, perfect in truthfulness … perfect in everything!"[21]

She goes on to say:

> *We should be in awe of God for who He is—because He is God. And we should admire God because of what He is like. This is the fear of the Lord—being in awe of God because He is God, and admiring God because of the kind of person He is.*
>
> *To fear the Lord—to admire God because of what He is like—is also to trust Him. We know we can trust Him because He is perfect in power and perfect in love for His children.*[22]

We talked in the first chapter about the Israelites, God's chosen people. He revealed His greatness as He set His rescue plan in motion with miraculous displays of power and might: rivers that parted into dry pathways, manna and quail raining down their daily bread, enemy armies toppling, and water spurting out of rocks in the desert.

The command to fear God was wrapped in the comforting warmth of trust in His provision, sweet rest in His perfect goodness, and exquisite joy at being loved and chosen.

Isn't that awesome? Believers are grafted in, adopted into God's family, and we, too, are chosen as God's beloved. We do not earn God's favor. His love is a gift.

This God, this great creator who holds all of earth together and is unspeakably beautiful and perfect, this set-apart holy One who we stand in utmost awe of ... this God chose us. He loves us!

Sally Michael says, "God is an amazing lover of people who don't deserve to be loved. Does that amaze you? Part of what it means to fear the Lord is to be amazed by God's love."[23]

1 John 4:18 actually tells us, "Perfect love casts out fear."

Here is where the rivers of love and fear meet in a rushing waterfall of grace.

Perfect love slept in a hay-strewn manger, and hammered nails alongside His earthly papa. Perfect love was tempted to sin in a lonely desert, and battled the enemy of our souls with weapons of Scripture and inner strength. Perfect love was baptized in the Jordan River, and the voice of God proclaimed His Son-ship. Perfect love healed the sick, touched the untouchables, and taught the masses with patience and authority. Perfect love died on the cross and rose again after three days.

It is a wonder that Jesus came, and that He carried our sin to the cross. His love for us is amazing! He died so that the holy one could touch sinners. So that broken, failing humans could share eternity with God the perfect.

He died so that terror-fear could mingle with mercy and become reverent, protected, awed-by-love devotion to God!

Wow!

Fear in the knees-knocking, tongue-tying, head-covering, trembling to the tips of our fingers sense is banished by the love of God that sweeps in, breathtaking and sacrificial, in the gospel story. The new fear is a soul-deep amazement, that the God who breathed creation to life actually loves His people so much that He became one of them! Jehovah God is also Emmanuel, God with us! The God who struck fear into the hearts of His enemies came low and knelt humble to love us.

The love of God towards sinners is unfathomable. Spread your arms wide and try to gather as much of the beauty as you can as we dive into its depths.

1 John 4:8 says, "Anyone who does not love does not know God, because God is love."

God is love. No qualifications. The very essence of God is love! His other attributes radiate from the core of His being: His love.

The love of God was, according to Wayne Grudem, "... active even before creation among the members of the Trinity. Jesus speaks to his Father of 'my glory which you have given me in your love for me before the foundation of the world' (John 17:24), thus indicating that there was love and giving of honor from the Father to the Son from all eternity."[24]

God the Father declared Jesus to be "my beloved son," on the day He was baptized by John. And Jesus affirmed His love for the Father by His obedience. He submitted to every command of God, drank the bitter cup placed before Him, and obeyed God even unto death. John 14:31 tells us that He did so in order that the world would know the love He had for His Father.

The concept of the Trinity can be a complicated thought to grasp. But when you think about perfect love existing in the deep void of time before creation, it makes sense that God is both one and three, doesn't it? One holy God, yet three Persons to enact the fullness of His character. Love existed because relationship existed. In perfect harmony, the Father, the Son, and the Holy Spirit existed, loved, and created. God's love—manifested in a flawless synchrony between the Persons of the Trinity—was then extended to created man.

There was love inherent in God even before Adam's clay-formed nostrils flared and breath exhaled from his lungs. God chose to create, and He chose to bestow His affection on His creation.

And so we watch the great story unfold: the breaking, and then the redeeming. God's love never wavered, never stopped, even as His people turned away from Him, over and over and over. We see God's people in bondage, then rescued, then wandering, then victorious. Then, defeated. In bondage again. And God's loving kindness is woven, bright and silken, through every story.

To Moses, God proclaimed, "The Lord, the Lord, a God merciful and gracious, slow to anger and abounding in steadfast love and faithfulness" (Exodus 34:6).

Psalm 36:5 and 7 say, "Your steadfast love, O Lord, extends to the heavens, your faithfulness to the clouds … How precious is your steadfast love, O God! The children of mankind take refuge in the shadow of your wings."

Psalm 136:26 adds, "Give thanks to the God of heaven, for his steadfast love endures forever."

God's love is steadfast, faithful, and everlasting. His unswerving devotion to His beloved compelled Him to, at just the right time, send His Son as the Savior of His people. He implanted the essence of His Son within Mary's womb, and Jesus grew, a tiny, love-filled miracle, within her. We celebrate His birth at Christmas, with our hearts and eyes fixed down the road at Easter.

He came as a baby, so He could live a sinless life, and so He could die the death we deserve.

My children love to recite John 3:16. I think we have memorized the words set to four or five different tunes, and we each have our favorites. You know what? I never get tired of hearing their sweet soprano voices sing these words: "For God so loved the world, that he gave his only Son, that whoever believes in him should not perish but have eternal life."

I think we can grow too accustomed to the love of God, sometimes. We forget how awesome it is to be loved by God, completely in spite of ourselves and our blunders. His love is so boundless, so amazing. We don't deserve to be loved that way! We cannot earn the favor of God. He chose us, and that should fill us with absolute wonder. We are sinners, and God the perfect One loves us! He sent His Son to be born in a stable, to live among common people, to touch sinners with His stunning mercy.

His love is no ordinary love. His love *defines* love.

Do you see what He did for us? Do you "see what kind of love the Father has lavished upon us, that we should be called the children of God?" (1 John 3:1).

Tonight, as I swept grains of rice from my kitchen floor and scrubbed dirty dishes at my sink, I sang Stuart Townend's song, "How Deep the Father's Love for Us." I probably sang off-key. But the words of the song lifted my heart beyond the mundane task of tidying the kitchen after another meal. They reminded me of God's love, and my heart soared.

> *"How deep the Father's love for us,*
> *How vast beyond all measure,*
> *That He should give His only Son*
> *To make a wretch His treasure.*
> *How great the pain of searing loss -*
> *The Father turns His face away,*

As wounds which mar the Chosen One
Bring many sons to glory."[25]

God is worthy of our adoration. His power, His goodness, His sovereignty, and His holiness all compel us to stand in awe, to be amazed. And His love, oh, His love. It softens cowering hearts into deeply bowed ones. The love of God entwines His other attributes with a ribbon of pure beauty. His love bids us enter into the close relationship of Father and adopted children. His love prompts us to approach Him "with confidence" (Hebrews 4:16) in unceasing prayer. He is our God, and He is also our closest friend, our loving daddy.

The love of God did not stop at salvation. He poured out His love for us in a letter. The Bible is God's gift of love to us, isn't it? His grace and kindness allowed us to have a book to read and hold and study. We are able to know God through His word, and we are blessed to learn His ways, that we might walk in them. God rained love on us when He gave believers the Holy Spirit, too. He sent us a Comforter for our journey. The Holy Spirit lives in us, enables us, and gives grace and power to our daily outworking of faith.

It would have been enough for Christ to suffer on our behalf. But God kept going, kept dazzling us with love, equipping us for life on earth. He walks with us, intimately involved in every detail of our days. He gave us the gift of prayer, of talking with Him moment by moment as we wrestle through the trials and decisions of life. I can cry out to God in the middle of the night when a child is sick and I am at my wit's end. I can ask for wisdom when I struggle with severe discipline issues or even simple decisions about how to order and structure my children's days. God didn't just save us from our sins, although that would have been grace enough! He loves us so much He shares in our everyday lives through His word, through prayer, and through the strengthening mercy of His spirit at work in our hearts.

This is a God to love. And this is also a God to fear.

The fear of God looks like bowed reverence. It looks like a child, restrained by the fearsome and protective authority of her father. It looks like a bride, bedazzled by the alluring love of her husband.

As we grow in our understanding of who God is, and of how unfathomable it is that He has chosen to love us deeply, individually, and irrevocably, the right kind of fear will grow in our hearts. We will fear God alone, and His love will cast out every other fear.

Psalm 128:1 proclaims, "Blessed is everyone who fears the Lord, who walks in His ways!" God promises blessing when our hearts belong wholly to Him, and our lives are patterned after His righteousness.

In two weeks, my two older daughters will attend school outside of our home for the first time. I chose a verse for each of them as their special school verses, verses for them to hold on to as they face new challenges in a new classroom. I decorated construction paper with scrolling letters and simple drawings in marker (I mentioned I'm not artistic, right?) and posted the verses on their bedroom wall to be a daily reminder of the Lord's guidance in their lives.

My eight-year-old, Elisa, was thrilled that the key word in her verse is "joy." After all, her middle name is Joy! I read her the verse, and shared with her that the Lord desires for her to follow whole-heartedly after Him, and that when she sets her feet firmly on His path, she will experience His sweet, down-deep, unstoppable joy. She doesn't quite grasp what it means to fear the Lord right now (we haven't gotten to that chapter yet in Sally Michael's devotional), but as she grows she will begin to understand that fearing God is a part of following His path. And her special verse will gain even richer meaning.

Psalm 16:11 says, "You make known to me the path of life; in your presence there is fullness of joy; at your right hand are pleasures forevermore."

A right fear and adoration of God will enable us to shrug off the weight of man-fearing we carry. We will learn to walk light as recipients of His grace—and to make pleasing and enjoying God our highest aim. The path of life that once seemed so strenuous and burdensome will be eased by the comforting presence of our God, and He will lavish us with the fullness of His joy!

◈

During the year that my husband and I dated, we discovered our tastes in both music and movies were virtually incompatible. He liked explosions, excitement, and cowboys. I liked *Anne of Green Gables.* He listened to incoherent, loud (mostly Christian) rock, and country music. I preferred the melodic strains of more mellow Christian music, and soft instrumental themes. One day, as we were driving together on Whidbey Island, near Seattle, I happened to insert a *Third Day* CD. Erik smiled, and sang along. I sang along, too, and from that moment on, *Third Day's* tunes were our music of choice whenever we were together.

We have since discovered a few other crossover choices. We both enjoy jazz, for instance, and I have grown to appreciate some older country artists. But, *Third Day* is still our favorite, and accordingly, we have memorized quite a few of their lyrics.

As I have written this chapter, I have been listening often to the song, "King of Glory." In fact, I've been playing it on repeat in the car. My kids don't seem to mind.

It seems fitting to close this chapter with these poignant lyrics.

> *"Who is this King of Glory that pursues me with His love*
> *And haunts me with each hearing of His softly spoken words*
> *My conscience, a reminder of forgiveness that I need*
> *Who is this King of Glory who offers it to me*
> *Who is this King of angels, O blessed Prince of Peace*

Revealing things of heaven and all its mysteries
My spirit's ever longing for His grace in which to stand
Who is this King of Glory, Son of God and son of man
His name is Jesus, precious Jesus
The Lord Almighty, the King of my heart
The King of glory
Who is this King of Glory with strength and majesty
And wisdom beyond measure, the gracious King of kings
the Lord of Earth and heaven, the Creator of all things
Who is this King of Glory, He's everything to me
The Lord of Earth and heaven, the Creator of all things
He is the King of Glory, He's everything to me."[26]

CHAPTER SIX:
Clothed in His Righteousness

It's 10:45 on a Tuesday morning. According to the schedule printed and tacked to the side of the schoolroom bookshelf, we should be practicing our weekly memory work now. Singing our timeline song and doing jumping jacks as we recite Latin verb endings.

But we're not. Instead, a child is screaming about math. It should have been done an hour ago, but a series of attitude flare-ups and small frustrations have now spiraled into a whirling tornado of misplaced anger. My little girl is a mess. The math is not difficult for her, but the timer on her drill beeped too early, and she furiously blamed a sister whose nearby play disrupted her thinking. I tried to help her shrug it off. It doesn't matter, but, oh, in her little heart, it does! I asked her to skip a tough section until I was available to help her. It was time for me to focus on helping her preschool-age sister with letter sounds and stories. Angry, she hurled the math paper onto the floor. When I asked her to pick it up and move to another room, a hard, thick black pencil line scarred the page with her fury.

So now she screams. Me? I gouge my lip with my teeth, biting back tears. What do I do?

My wild one goes to her room, stomping loud and enraged, at my request. I need to pray. She needs a break. She's not teachable, and I don't know where to go from here.

I set my other kiddos up with worksheets and books and toys, and I trail her up the stairs. I pray, kneading my temples, and I let a single tear fall.

Finally, I remember what I need to pray. "God, how does the truth of your gospel meet us here, in the ugly mess of this moment?" I say the words aloud, entering her bedroom with soft footsteps and a broken heart.

I climb up onto her bunk-bed, move aside the now-crumpled math page, and I lay beside my tall, lanky girl with the doe brown eyes and the fiery heart.

I stroke her hair, and I am quiet for a moment. I kiss her cheek, taste her salty tears, too. "Sweet girl," I breathe. "What's going on? What is this about?"

She doesn't know, and I have to pry hard. We talk about the anger, about the inappropriateness of it, about how the Bible teaches that a fool gives vent to his anger, but the wise man is self-controlled. We talk about whether her anger was righteous, or whether she was merely angry because her desires were thwarted. We talk about authority, and how I am hers, given to her by God. We talk about responsibility and work, and how we are to do our work as unto the Lord. I show her the ruined math page, and ask if it is work she can present to the Lord. She murmurs, grumbles, shakes her head. We talk about sin.

And, then, me still stroking her forehead, rubbing her back, we talk about Jesus. We talk about His perfect record, about how He came, and lived, perfectly, without sin. How He died, our sin heaped on Him at the cross. And, in that moment, He paid the price for our sin. He took it, and He redeemed us, and He handed us back a new record in exchange for our sin-stained one. He was never angry unless it was a righteous anger at sin, and now, even though she has spent the morning with anger full-throttle, she has His record!

"That's grace, honey," I whisper. "Praise God that He sent us a Savior!"

I preach the gospel to her on her bunk-bed, and I pray, and then we go, hand-in-hand, back to the schoolroom. The scrawls of graphite on the math sheet are erased, and I sit with her as we work through the problems together. It still takes a while.

I am thankful for the gospel. I preach it to my struggling daughter, and I hear it in my own heart. I forget, often, how precious it is, how needed it is. I forget to tell myself who I belong to, and who I am because of His grace.

My little struggling sweetheart needed to know, even in her moment of abhorrent behavior, that she is forgiven and renewed because Jesus has washed away her sin and given her new life. She is loved and she is lovely—because of Him.

In case you haven't heard it lately, let's delve deeper into the truth of our identity in Christ. Who are we, in Him? In spite of the sin that dirties our hearts? In spite of all the right things we know to do and yet fail to do, every time? In spite of our worthless efforts to be good apart from Christ?

A right view of God is paramount as we begin to let go of the weighty bundles strapped to our lives. And so is a right view of ourselves. Through a lens of biblical truth, we need to see ourselves as beloved sons and daughters, redeemed and restored by Christ's blood.

God knows us. Have you stopped to consider that, lately? In a sea of millions—nay, billions—we are each individually and completely known by our creator. I have an impossibly thick and wiry head of hair, and the Bible tells me God has counted each and every one of my wavy, brownish strands (Matthew 10:30). Isaiah 49:16 tells us our names our engraved on the palm of His hand.

I was one of those little girls who filled notebooks with creative, beautiful names I wanted to give to my future babies. I also wrote fiction, and the runner-up names often became characters in my stories. I have loved choosing names for our four children. It hasn't always been easy for my husband

and me to agree on those choices, I will admit. In fact, during the last few weeks of my third pregnancy, Erik went on a mission trip to Kenya, and his parting words (aside from "I love you!") were, "If you have the baby—and if it's a girl, then name her Raina. If it's a boy, then, man, I don't know. You'll just have to wait." We could not settle on a name that meshed my qualification of a strong and valiant meaning with his qualification of a strong and valiant sound. Thankfully, it was a girl, and Raina (a Hebrew name meaning *song of the Lord*) Abigail (*her father's joy*) was born a full week and a half after Erik returned from Africa.

Names matter, and our Lord has etched ours into His palm. He knows us by name; He has claimed us. I am not just an invisible speck on His great globe. He knows who I am, and He knows who you are.

He knows us because He made us.

Psalm 139:13-16 says this. "For you formed my inward parts; you knitted me together in my mother's womb. I praise you, for I am fearfully and wonderfully made. Wonderful are your works; my soul knows it very well. My frame was not hidden from you, when I was being made in secret, intricately woven in the depths of the earth. Your eyes saw my unformed substance; in your book were written, every one of them, the days that were formed for me, when as yet there was none of them."

The privilege of carrying new life in my own womb has filled my spirit with unspeakable awe each time. Two lines on a white pregnancy test strip. A baby! A kidney-bean sized miracle. The wonder of all that takes place within a woman when the Lord fills her womb with His gift of life is amazing! I would touch my belly when it was still soft and flat—when there was no tell-tale roundness to prove the growth of my minute miracle. I would imagine what the Lord was doing, what He had already done. I couldn't see inside to witness the careful weaving, the pairing of chromosomes and the pulsing of blood, the shaping of a placenta, a cord, a body. But, God saw! "My frame was not hidden from you," verse 15 says, "when I was being made in secret." With a few of our pregnancies, we guarded our secret for twelve or more weeks. No one besides my husband and I knew that my nauseated tummy held a precious, growing baby. The aching weariness that overtook my body was caused by a pea-sized secret, and I marveled at what was taking place within me, unbeknownst to anyone!

Isn't it amazing? Every new life is hand-formed by God! When that baby is still no bigger than a kiwi, or an egg (seems like we always used food terminology to describe our babies to our older children), He has already written the story of his or her life. He already knows everything about His child, and He loves him or her!

The earlier part of Psalm 139 tell us, "O Lord, you have searched me and known me! You know when I sit down and when I rise up; you discern my thoughts from afar. You search out my path and my lying down and are acquainted with all my ways. Even before a word is on my tongue, behold, O Lord, you know it altogether. You hem me in, behind and before, and lay your hand upon me. Such knowledge is too wonderful for me; it is high; I cannot attain it" (verses 1-6).

Like King David, I cannot attain such knowledge. I can't grasp it. How is it that God knows us so intimately? Each of us? Every one of the millions and billions. Can you marvel with me at that for a minute?

"When I look at your heavens, the work of your fingers, the moon and the stars, which you have set in place, what is man that you are mindful of him, and the son of man that you care for him?" David asks in Psalm 8:3-4.

God knows my heart. He knows the tender areas of my soul that I hide with a strong front so I can look like I have it all together. He knows my quirks and my idiosyncrasies; He laughs kindly at my silliness. He knows the way I fidget when I'm nervous, and the way my voice gets high and squeaky when I talk on the phone. He knows I fumble clumsy when it comes to practical skills like home maintenance and gardening—or even crocheting, but I can make melt-in-your-mouth cookies without a recipe. He knows that I'd far prefer to open a stack of new books on Christmas morning than unwrap the keys to a new car (not that that would ever happen!). He knows that scented candles and empty notebooks make me happy, and He knows that dirty countertops make me crazy. He knows my fears—the deep worries that settle heavy in my heart. He knows the depth and breadth of who I am. And, He knows the depth and breadth of who you are, too.

Our little girls are growing up without Santa Claus. Sure, they love the movie *The Polar Express*, and we have a homemade, fluffy cloth copy of *The Night Before Christmas*, but Santa Claus has never been a part of our family Christmas celebrations. They know he is pretend, a fanciful legend based on the true story of the generous Saint Nicholas. Even though it would be fun to leave a plate of cookies on the coffee table for Santa, or to lie awake listening for the patter of reindeer hooves on the roof, I believe there are good reasons for keeping Santa out of Christmas.

The legends tell us that Santa knows all about the comings and goings of the world's children. He is watching, waiting, to see if boys and girls are bad or good. He knows, in fact, when they are asleep, and when they are awake! Just like the Lord, who knows the lying down and the waking of His beloved children. The difference, though, is this. Santa only gives gifts to those who are good. In the Christmas legend, he is keeping an eye out for the purpose of discriminating between good and bad children. While the good boys and girls receive shiny-wrapped gifts, the ones who have messed up too many times only receive a lump of coal in the bottoms of their expectantly hung stockings.

That is not like our God. His purposes at Christmas are vastly different. Jesus came to offer the free Christmas gift of salvation to us because we were bad, and we needed it!

In God's mindfulness of us as His created beings, He also knows our weaknesses. He knows we are born into sin; He knows the frailty and the ugliness of our unregenerate souls.

"For He knows our frame," Psalm 103:14 says. "He remembers that we are dust." Adam was formed from dust, and mankind decomposes into dirt after our physical death. We are small and we are sinful in the presence of our everlasting Lord.

Are you ever aware of your own sinfulness in a particularly cognizant way? Just this morning, as I sat at a quiet table, looking out on a misty morning, and wrapping my bare legs in a quilt to chase off the chill from the open window, my mind dwelled on the mistakes of yesterday. The words spoken in haste, the self-focus that led to awkwardness, the opportunities lost and the moments spent rushing instead of dwelling. I saw my neediness before the Lord, and remembered that apart from His grace, I cannot live well. I cannot glorify Him in my own strength. I cannot be the mother, the wife, or the Christ-follower I long to be without His covering. So I prayed for His indwelling. I prayed I would stop striving in my own might and walk bravely into the unknown beyond—so His grace, love, and power could be displayed in my life.

We need Jesus!

We have alluded to the gospel story many times throughout this book. Most likely, you would not have read this far if you did not have a relationship with God and long to walk more closely with Him. Yet, a discussion of our identity in Christ must contain a clear picture of His atonement for us on the cross. The cross carries us from the doomed mess of our sinful lives to the promise of eternity in heaven, and into the position of adopted sons and daughters of God! Will you allow me to walk us—briefly—through the gospel? If you are a believer, then this is the good story, the one we ought to never tire of hearing or proclaiming. And if you have never heard the truth of what God has done for you, then I pray these words would make the gospel beautiful to you, that you would see His kindness and fall in love with the one who loved you first!

Remember the fall? Remember the undoing, the unraveling, the rupture of all that was good and perfect in God's original creation? Remember God had a plan to redeem all of it?

Salvation by substitutionary atonement was His plan, and here is how He carried it out. He waited, revealing Himself through Old Testament history and showing mankind our needfulness of a Savior through laws that could never be perfectly kept. And then, He sent Jesus. His Son. Jesus, fully God and fully man, was born in a cattle stall in Bethlehem and lived a humble, obscure existence as the son of an unknown carpenter. As a baby, He and His parents sought temporary refuge in Egypt before settling down to life in the small town of Nazareth. At the age of thirty, Jesus performed His first miracle, and began a three-year earthly ministry. He healed, He loved, He gave, and He taught. A band of ragamuffin followers kept company with Him, learning His ways and experiencing His love.

As His ministry became more visible and His followers became more plentiful, Jesus incurred the ire, derision, and fear of the Jewish leaders. Jesus was betrayed by one of His disciples, tried as a criminal, and eventually sentenced to death on a cross.

His crucifixion was the fulfillment of God's plan to atone—once and for all—for the sin of humanity. At the cross, Jesus lay down His life, gave up His spirit, and experienced the rending of His eternal union with God the Father. He suffered immense physical pain, and tortuous mental separation from His Father as He willingly surrendered His life. Nails pierced His hands and feet, a crown of spiky thorns adorned His princely head, and the weight of the world was literally rained down upon His bloody shoulders.

Why did Jesus—who could have summoned angels to His aid, who could have bounded down from the cross with an easy leap—submit to such a horrific death?

Because sin requires punishment. There is a penalty for our wrongdoing and it must be paid. Under the old covenant, sins were atoned for by never-ending animal sacrifices. The shedding of blood paid the price—for a time. But, no sooner had the priests atoned for the sins of that day than God's followers would fail again. Stumbling, staggering beneath the impossible standards, they had to repeat the cycle again and again.

Jesus is the only one who could keep God's law. He is the only one who could live a perfect life, who could fight temptation and win—every time.

So, perfect in every way, an unblemished Lamb, Jesus—our God and our King—was able to atone for our sins. He was the forever sacrifice—the once and for all atonement. No more lambs. No more goats. Just Jesus, God and man, who loved us enough, and loved His Father enough, to submit to death on a cross. He willingly gave His life as the perfect, sacrificial Lamb, and He died our death.

Maybe this doesn't seem beautiful to you. Maybe it seems messy, or bloody, or strange. Maybe it even seems unnecessary. But when we see God as high and holy, then we understand why sin cannot be a part of Him. Why *we* cannot be a part of Him. His perfect, set-apart holiness cannot be one with sin. But God loved us—so He made a way. Not a plan B, but a plan—a wildly generous plan that involved sending His own Son to suffer and die on our behalf. Jesus' death was God's plan unfurled. It was His mercy poured out. His love bestowed. We can be united with Christ because He died for us.

And because He rose for us! Let's not leave out this most important piece! Sunday morning! Jesus lay in a tomb, sealed and still, for three days. But God did not just send His Son to die; He sent Him to conquer death itself. On the morning of the third day, Jesus rose! His lungs inhaled and exhaled again; His legs held the weight of His body as He stood up and shed the burial rags. The stone barring the entrance to the tomb was rolled away as an earthquake shook the ground.

Jesus won! He died to pay the penalty for our sin. He rose victorious over death in order to give us newness of life. Because Jesus was God, death had no hold on Him. And because we are one with Him in His sacrifice, death also has no hold on us.

This is the gospel. Jesus lived, He died, and He rose—all for obedience to His Father and love for lost sinners.

We have hope, because in Jesus' death our sins are atoned for; our punishment was heaped on the perfect one. We have hope, because in Jesus' resurrection, the power of sin and death were conquered.

Romans 4:25 tells us Jesus "was delivered up for our trespasses and raised for our justification."

And in chapter 5 of that same book, Paul goes on to say: "For while we were still weak, at the right time Christ died for the ungodly. For one will scarcely die for a righteous person—though perhaps for a good person one would even dare to die—but God shows His love for us in that while we were still sinners, Christ died for us. Since, therefore, we have now been justified by His blood, much more shall we be saved by Him from the wrath of God" (verses 6-9).

What must we do to be forgiven? What is required of us in order to inherit eternal life with God? To be justified by His blood?

The answer, in its simplest form, is nothing. There is no active work which we must accomplish in order to achieve salvation. Rather, salvation is about Jesus awakening our spirits to new life, about Him stirring within our hearts a longing for Him, about Jesus drawing us to Himself and giving us a desire to trust Him! It is not until the Holy Spirit has gently tugged on our spiritually dormant hearts we are able to even believe! John 6:44 says, "No one can come to me unless the Father who sent me draws him..."

For belief in Christ is all that is required of us in order to be saved! John 20:31 tells us the words of John were written for the purpose of belief—"but these are written so that you may believe that Jesus is the Christ, the Son of God, and that by believing you may have life in his name."

Paul tells the Romans, "For I am not ashamed of the gospel, for it is the power of God for salvation to everyone who believes ..." (Romans 1:16).

Ephesians 2:8 says, "For by grace you have been saved through faith. And this is not your own doing; it is the gift of God."

This saving belief in Jesus is a conscious belief. It is a trust in His sacrifice for the covering of our sins, and a dependence on His death to cleanse us—personally—from our sins. It involves a deep sorrow, a repentance, for the sins He paid for with His life. And when we make that decision of mind and soul, when we receive His grace—offered as a gift from His outstretched hands—a miracle takes place within our hearts.

Once, we were dead in our sins. "But God, being rich in mercy, because of the great love with which He loved us, even when we were dead in our trespasses, made us alive together with Christ – by grace you have been saved – and raised us up with him and seated us with him in the heavenly places in Christ Jesus, so that in the coming ages He might show the immeasurable riches of His grace in kindness towards us in Christ Jesus" (Ephesians 2:4-7).

The fall had deadened our hearts—but salvation gives us new life in Christ!

Scripture refers to spiritual conversion as "rebirth." Jesus told Nicodemus that "unless one is born of water and the Spirit, he cannot enter the kingdom of God" (John 3:5).

Even the Old Testament foreshadowed the coming spiritual regeneration. Ezekiel 36:26-27 says, "And I will give you a new heart, and a new spirit

I will put within you. And I will remove the heart of stone from your flesh and give you a heart of flesh. And I will put my Spirit within you, and cause you to walk in my statutes and be careful to obey my rules."

When the Lord draws our spirits to Him, and we respond with heart-felt faith in His work on the cross, we are given new life, a new heart. We are born again! Peter tells us, "You have been born anew, not of perishable seed but of imperishable, through the living and abiding word of God" (1 Peter 1:23). And in 2 Corinthians 5:17, we read, "If anyone is in Christ, he is a new creation; the old has passed away, behold the new has come."

There have been sections of this book that have felt weighty (even to me, as I write). We have talked about sin, and idolatry, and the worthlessness of our own feeble efforts at righteousness. If some of those topics have bowed you down, heavy, then I pray these next sections feel a bit like the gentle tipping upward of your chin. I want to look you in the eyes and tell you who are *in Christ.*

At the cross, a truly remarkable, once-and-for-all transaction occurred. Remember that fancy word we used? Christ *justified* us. We no longer stand before God as condemned sinners, with a track record of struggle and shame. Christ has written His name over our hearts, and His perfection has been transferred to us. That was the grace I whispered over my math-angry daughter during our Tuesday morning showdown, and it's the grace I whisper to myself when the voice of condemnation haunts my sin-weary heart.

In Christ, you are redeemed. In Him, you are beautiful! All those fears of being exposed, of not measuring up, of being rejected? They melt away, because the grace of God has birthed new life in us, and we are not measured by standards of earthly goodness. We are measured by the standard of Christ and His perfection, which He has transferred to us!

2 Corinthians 5:21 says, "For our sake he made him to be sin who knew no sin, so that in him we might become the righteousness of God."

My sweet daughters love butterflies. Several years ago, we visited a butterfly garden in South Dakota. We entered a sultry, glass-encased room that stole your breath with its tropical warmth. Hundreds of vibrant-hued dancers fluttered and twirled from plant to flower, sometimes pausing to rest fragile wings on fingertips or shoelaces. We marveled. We stood stock-still to wonder at colors and details and beauty. A lepidopterist (isn't that a fun word?) released newly emerged butterflies from a wooden cage in the corner, gesturing to a room behind her where caterpillars formed chrysalises and gently incubated before bursting forth in flight.

Our life in Christ is similar to the metamorphosis of the caterpillar. We are creeping caterpillars, bland and dull, unable to fly. Then, Jesus saves us. He stirs our hearts, calls us to repentance, and awakens spiritual life within us. He endows us with His beauty, His radiance. And He summons us from our cocoons—free to fly in His glorious strength.

The Bible calls us children of God. We are no longer "sons of disobedience" (Ephesians 2:2). Rather, our allegiance is now with Christ. John 1:12 says, "But to all who did receive him, who believed in his name, he gave the right to become children of God, who were born, not of blood nor of the will of the flesh nor of the will of man, but of God."

My father passed away seven years ago. At the time I was eight months pregnant with my daughter Sadie; only my oldest daughter had the sweet privilege of knowing her tender, strong Boppa. My daddy was soft-spoken, but loud in laughter. His laughter rumbled through his thick chest and shook his broad shoulders. He was the most kind and patient man I have ever known, although he spoke the truth firmly when he needed to. I remember as a little girl loving to latch my arms and legs around his ankles, hanging on for a wild ride around the house. I remember hearing his footsteps enter the brick entryway at dinnertime and running for a scratchy-cheeked hug. I remember hearing his voice booming loud from the sidelines of a track meet or a volleyball game as he cheered for his kiddos. My daddy was not perfect, but he loved us well. I have only a few pictures of Dad with Elisa, and they are precious to me: her snuggled in his lap for a story, his arms holding her fragile newborn body, him pulling her on a sled during her first winter. I miss my dad, but I miss him with a thankful heart. I was blessed with a daddy who lavished love, encouragement, and acceptance on his children. I know not every child is given such a gift.

But we have a Father in heaven who offers His perfect love to each and every one of us! God welcomes us into His spiritual family and calls us His children.

Romans 8:14-16 says, "For all who are led by the Spirit of God are sons of God. For you did not receive the spirit of slavery to fall back into fear, but you have received the Spirit of adoption as sons, by whom we cry, 'Abba! Father!' The Spirit himself bears witness with our spirit that we are children of God, and if children, then heirs—heirs of God and fellow heirs with Christ, provided we suffer with him in order that we may also be glorified with him."

John MacArthur describes the word "Abba" as an "informal Aramaic term for Father that conveys a sense of intimacy. Like the English terms 'Daddy' or 'Papa,' it connotes tenderness, dependence, and a relationship free of fear of anxiety."[27]

I am a grown-up now. And my own daddy is in heaven. But it still warms my heart to imagine the intimacy invited by God when He gives us the privilege of calling Him Papa! Like my brother and sisters and I ran to the front door to engulf our papa in joyful embraces, God wants us to run open-armed to Him. He wants us to climb in His lap and rest with Him, to know His comforting love. He wants to tenderly pat our heads, ruffling the hairs He has counted, assuring us of His never-ending love. My husband loves it when our girls call him Papa. "Dad" is a fine term—and it's the one they use when they need his help, when they have a question, or when their play turns rough-and-tumble and teasing. Erik's heart melts, though, when a blonde-haired princess clambers into his lap, pats his bristly chin, and declares, "I love you, Papa." When I think of God inviting His followers to address Him as Papa, I am amazed at the tenderness of His love for us.

God loves you! If you have believed, then you are His child. He longs for you to run to Him with the happy abandon of a child, calling out "Papa" and receiving His warm and welcoming embrace.

Becoming a child of God has two important implications. The first is the comforting intimacy that we have been discussing: the joy and surety of having a mighty Papa in heaven. The second implication is what Romans 8:17 tells us, that if we are children, then we are heirs, "heirs of God and fellow heirs with Christ, provided we suffer with him in order that we may also be glorified with him."

Hebrews 1:2 tells us God has appointed His Son to be "the heir of all things." I don't have a complete understanding of all the Bible promises with regard to the coming new heaven and earth, but the Bible makes it clear that Jesus will ultimately rule over all things. And we are His co-heirs!

In Matthew 25:34, Jesus speaks about the final judgment, saying, "Then the King will say to those on his right, 'Come, you who are blessed by my Father, inherit the kingdom prepared for you from the foundation of the world.'"

Before the world was spoken into being, the triune God was preparing the future inheritance for His adopted sons and daughters.

Ephesians 1:11 -14 reads, "In him we have obtained an inheritance, having been predestined according to the purpose of him who works all things according to the counsel of his will, so that we who were the first to hope in Christ might be to the praise of his glory. In him you also, when you heard the word of truth, the gospel of your salvation, and believed in him, were sealed with the promised Holy Spirit, who is the guarantee of our inheritance until we acquire possession of it, to the praise of his glory."

What does all this mean? Why is it significant that God has named believers co-heirs with His Son? Again, God's kindness is extravagant. He could have chosen simply to rescue us from our eternal punishment in hell. But in the fullness of His grace, He didn't *just* rescue us. We were beggars, clothed in rags, tattered and tired and without hope. And God didn't just clothe us in simple, clean garments and hand us a plateful of nourishing food to fill our rumbling bellies. No, He wrapped us in royal robes. He led us to a banquet table spread with culinary delights and invited us to dine off the finest china plates. God didn't just save us. He raised us up out of our lowly place, and He welcomed us with unabashed, fatherly love. He saw the perfect record of Christ in us, and He called us His sons and daughters, too. The inheritance of God is shared between Christ and the Church.

We inherit salvation. We inherit the forever reward of heaven. We get to be with God, be one with Him. The verse in Ephesians tells us that the Holy Spirit is set as a seal on our hearts, the promise within us to guarantee our eternal inheritance. We inherit life with God! An intimate relationship we don't deserve is offered to us through Christ. We stand secure, by God's grace, in the righteousness of Christ.

And in a befuddling twist of boundless mercy, we are also somehow heirs of God's glory, and heirs to all of the created universe, which will be remade, renewed, and ruled by Jesus after He returns and defeats the power of Satan finally and forever.

Whew! How is that possible? How is it that broken sinners are so gifted with God's grace that we are even promised a share of His inheritance? God's economy does not make sense to our human minds, does it? His love is beyond our understanding, and His grace is more than amazing.

That God deems to call us His children ... that He loves us, and delights in us, and showers us with such heavenly treasures ... these truths ought to touch our hearts, transform us, and ignite our spirits to worship.

⟨◇⟩

White lace frames the glowing face of the bride as she clutches the elbow of her father. A fitted gown of shimmering satin cascades to the floor, then trails behind her in a swooping white train. Ringlets of long hair brush her shoulders beneath the veil's transparent covering. Her lips smile pink, and her eyes blink bright and glittery. She is pure loveliness, breathtaking, beautiful.

Strands of soft piano music accompany her slow entrance, the melody wafting over her and accentuating the sacred loveliness of her graceful steps. At the narthex of the church, her groom waits, entranced by her beauty. His eyes brim with unshed tears as he beholds the all-white purity of his lovely bride.

Her father kisses her cheek as he gently transfers her hand to her patient bridegroom. The groom beholds her, breathes the sweet, clean scent of her, takes in her beauty and can hardly believe she is to become his wife! Voices hushed with emotion, they pledge vows to one another, vows to love, to cherish, to have and to hold, until they are parted by death.

Have you attended a wedding recently? If you are married, do you remember how that moment felt? Do you remember the flushed headiness of walking down the aisle (or watching your beloved walk down the aisle), feeling beautiful and intoxicated with all wonder of being chosen for forever by the one you loved?

Well, the Bible also calls believers the bride of Christ.

In the book of Hosea, the nation of Israel is likened to a faithless and adulterous woman, an undeserving bride who is yet loved passionately and unconditionally by her husband.

Other Old Testament books also speak of God as the devoted husband and kinsman-redeemer of Israel.

Isaiah 54:5 says, "For your Maker is your husband, the Lord of hosts is his name; and the Holy One of Israel is your Redeemer, the God of the whole earth he is called."

The New Testament continues that word picture, describing our Lord as the husband and His church as the bride. But this bride has been redeemed, restored, and made beautiful by the sacrificial love of her husband. The bride—the church—is unworthy, a filthy peasant in ill-fitting clothes. But Jesus washes His church, He clothes her in a gown of purest silk, and He receives her in love.

Ephesians 5:25-27 says, "Husbands, love your wives, as Christ loved the church and gave himself up for her, that he might sanctify her, having cleansed her by the washing of water with the word, so that he might present the church to himself in splendor, without spot or wrinkle or any such thing, that she might be holy and without blemish."

In 2 Corinthians 11:2, Paul describes the "divine jealousy" he feels for the church in Corinth, "since I betrothed you to one husband, to present you as a pure virgin to Christ."

The book of Revelation tells us, in chapter 19, about the promised marriage feast, which occurs sometime after the rapture of believers, "Let us rejoice and exult and give him the glory, for the marriage of the Lamb has come, and his Bride has made herself ready; it was granted to her to clothe herself with fine linen, bright and pure – for the fine linen is the righteous deeds of the saints" (verses 7 and 8).

In heaven, marriage in the earthly fashion will not exist. I will not be wed to my husband for eternity. We will instead be united, together with Christ, and our union with Him will be so satisfying that we will never wish for the earthly prototype. Godly marriage on earth is intended as a portrait of Jesus' sacrificial love. It is intended to put the gospel on display—to model sacrifice, love, and submission between a husband who lays down his life for his bride, and a wife who serves, adores, and respects her husband. If it seems strange to consider our union with Christ as a marriage, it is because earthly marriage is meant to caricature the ultimate, heavenly oneness we will share with Christ, and not the other way around. It is not that our relationship with Jesus will one day resemble the pattern of marriage we have experienced on earth. Rather, our earthly marriages are mere shadows of the perfect marriage between Christ and His redeemed bride.

Here on earth, we think we know how to celebrate. We decorate ballrooms with ribbons, lights, and flowers. We set tables with sterling silver and clinking crystal. We line buffet tables with creative, beautifully arranged food. We toast, we dance, and we sing.

But no high school prom, or birthday party, no wedding reception or formal Christmas party can even begin to compare with the feast we are promised on the day our eternal vows with Christ are spoken. We are invited to the premier celebration of all time! We were created for this union, and we will celebrate with our Savior, our Husband, our God, as we worship Him and give Him glory!

My wedding dress is hanging in a closet in our home, zipped into a thick plastic garment bag. There are a few tatters along the bottom hem; I danced with uncharacteristically light feet on that night of all nights. I love that gown. When I put it on in the dressing room and saw the waterfall of satin layers that draped diagonally to the floor, I knew it was *my* wedding dress. So often, I look into the mirror and I count my flaws. I see the blemishes, the sags, the wrinkles. On our wedding day, I looked into the mirror and I saw beauty reflected. The bride is lovely. She just is. The love of the husband makes the bride radiant.

And the love of the Husband makes the church radiant! Collectively, the church is the eternal bride. Beautiful. Chosen. Garbed in the finest linen, the purest righteousness, we stand before Jesus as His beloved. He has chosen us, become one with us.

Our union with Jesus is our identity. This is who we are, in Him, because of His grace.

In Jesus, we are declared righteous. In Him, we are adopted into the family of God, and accorded all the riches of heaven. In Him, we are purified and presented as a spotless bride to the Prince of heaven and earth. We are given new hearts, and promised that one day the progressive sanctification of our earthly walks will culminate in a heavenly glorification.

How does our identity as believers change the way we think and live in the here and now? How does it equip us to navigate this rugged path between man-fearing to God-fearing?

Our fear of man is often a result of our desire to be approved of. Our identity is in our reputation, in what others think of us. Letting go of the burden of man-fearing involves supplanting that wrong identity with the truth of our identity in Jesus. We are not defined by what others think. We are defined by what God thinks.

He has declared us worthy because Jesus is worthy. We have attained His standard of holiness, not because of anything we have done, but because Jesus is holy. Everything we need for life and godliness is granted to us in Christ Jesus (2 Peter 1:3)! We do not need to crave the approval of man, because Jesus has garnered the approval of the Father on our behalf.

Of course, letting go of our heavy backpacks is not as simple as a mere shift in our thinking (although that is certainly a key component!). In the next chapter, we will slowly begin the process of shedding those ungodly fears. We will unfasten the buckles and lengthen the straps of our packs, so the weight will slide more easily off our weary shoulders. For now, take a moment and nestle snugly into the tender truth of what Jesus has done on your behalf. Rest in the comforting knowledge that He has paid the penalty for your sin, grafted you irrevocably into His family, and taken you as His bride. There is nothing you can do to add to His love for you!

CHAPTER SEVEN:
Loosening the Straps

Every Sunday after church, in the quiet space of babies' afternoon naps and older girls snuggled in with books and blankets, I sit at my kitchen table (yup, that one, the one with the nicks and stains all over its shabby white paint job). I unfold my weekly planner, sip milky tea, and dream up plans for the week ahead. I scrawl lists, etch in memory-making activities, write down particular books to read or games to play, choose dinner menus, and remind myself of appointments, tasks, and to-dos. For an hour, I think, pray, and jot down ideas. By the time my tea is drained to the last dark leaves, I have a plan. I am prepared for the week ahead. And while I hold my plans loosely, aware that the liveliness of a house with four children does not allow for rigid structure, that flexible guide is imperative to my sanity.

I admit it. I like lists. I like plans. My husband does too, although our lists look pretty different. Mine are hand-written, with neat little boxes for checking tasks off with pretty checkmarks. Erik uses computer spreadsheets. I don't even know how to make the kind of lists he creates, but he uses all sorts of mathematical tools to ensure accuracy on his lists.

Lists are good. Plans are good. And even though I said at the outset of this book I did not have a ten-step plan for finding freedom from the fear of man, I do think we need a plan of some sort! It is all well and good for me, as a mama, to hope my week at home is well-filled, with chores completed, meals prepared, and sweet moments shared with my little girls. But if I do not plan those elements into my week in a thoughtful and intentional way,

I will end the week disappointed. Likewise, it is all well and good for me to acknowledge my man-fearing tendencies and to think through the negative consequences of carrying this heavy backpack on my tired back, but if I don't take practical steps to shed the backpack, I will just be lugging it around with a sense of gnawing guilt in my spirit!

In this chapter, we will focus on some of the steps we need to take. Empowered by the Holy Spirit who indwells our hearts, we will loosen the straps that hold the weight of man-fearing so tightly against our backs.

Do you know what God says about the burden we are meant to carry?

In Matthew 11:28-30 Jesus says, "Come to me, all who labor and are heavy-laden, and I will give you rest. Take my yoke upon you and learn from me, for I am gentle and lowly in heart, and you will find rest for your souls. For my yoke is easy, and my burden is light."

God promises us rest from the endless struggle to achieve righteousness by ourselves. He promises an everlasting reprieve from striving and straining to be approved of through any other means than the grace of God. We rest in His grace, and our burdens become light.

There is a temptation in all of this to think we can simply hurl off the knapsack of man-fearing in one fell swoop, by adopting the stance of, "I am justified in Christ, so I don't have to care what others think!" It is a true statement, in one sense, right? We do not have to be defined by what others think. But placing our identity in Christ alone does not mean we stop caring! We must care! Saying "because I am justified in Christ, I don't have to care what others think," sounds a bit like Romans 6, where Paul asks, "What shall we say then? Are we to continue in sin that grace may abound?" Of course, the answer is no! Are we to live callously and without care, simply because we know we are justified in Christ?

Certainly not!

Rather, the motto we adopt should sound something like this: "I am found in Christ! Because He is living and working through me, I can be a minister of His love and grace to others. And because I have seen God's greatness, I desire His glory and not my own. I will not be swayed by fame or popularity or applause, but will instead seek to glorify the Lord in all that I say and do."

Easier said than done, right? As a writer and a word-lover, I know all too well that words can bend and twist and hide. We can say anything, but our lives bear the proof, don't they? Pretty words can be a shallow covering for our unchanged hearts, sometimes. I don't want my words to be white-wash. I want them to be true, sincere, and honestly reflective of both my inner life and the outward expressions of my faith. I want the words I wrote in that simple motto to ring true in every arena of my life. With all my heart, I want to desire only the glory of God. I long to crucify my flesh, be rid of self-focus, and love the Lord with all I am! I want to see the world the way God sees it, to share in His grief over sin, and His longing for the lost to be saved. I want to be a vessel through which He pours His love out on the world. Do you want that, too?

The difficulty comes in transferring a desire expressed in words into a life lived out in truth. I can say I don't want to carry the backpack anymore, but I have yet to remove the straps, drop it onto the dusty path, and watch it roll pell-mell down the side of the grassy hill.

The shoulder straps rub hard and the waistband pinches. It's time to let go of this ungainly, wrong-sized burden.

Click. Let's unbuckle the waistband to start with. Chapter Five was all about God—who is worthy of our fear and adoration because of who He is and what He has done. Are you filled with a holy reverence for who God is? Even though we have gone over what it means to rightly fear the Lord, I think this can be a sticking point. The buckle can be tight and tricky to unclasp. God must be big in our eyes in order for us to fear Him, but the reality is we don't see God tangibly in our everyday, earthly existence. We see His hand-iwork, yes. We see His divine intervention in our lives, and we read of His glory as we study Scripture. But God is not a looming physical presence. Because we don't see Him, we can sort of forget Him. Oh, we go to church, and we pray. But God seems distant, sometimes. We feel like we are looking at Him through a telescope instead of walking with Him hand in hand. He becomes small in our vision, and the people who are with us day-to-day, face-to-face, become large.

Do you see that in your life? God isn't visible, so my adoration of Him tends to shrink as the days go by and I immerse myself in the realities of earth. If I am not consistently reminding myself of His glory, then people become large (and in charge) in my life. I eagerly desire the approval of man, instead of following the advice of 2 Timothy 2:15, which says, "Do your best to present yourself to God as one approved, a worker who has no need to be ashamed, rightly handling the word of truth."

It's not man's approval I ought to seek, but in the nitty-gritty of real life, I sometimes forget who my first allegiance is to, whose kingdom my citizen-ship is truly in.

1 Thessalonians 2:4 also tells us, "But just as we have been approved by God to be entrusted with the gospel, so we speak, not to please man, but to please God who tests our hearts."

It is all too easy to snap the buckle of man-fearing back on because we forget how big and glorious God is and we begin to conform to the world around us, to desire the approval and pleasure of people. But if we have been approved by God through Jesus, we are called to speak (and live) in such a way that God is pleased—not man.

The first step to becoming a God-fearer is to learn (but not just once) how worthy He is. We must immerse ourselves in truth daily, so we will not forget and allow God's majesty to shrink in our hearts.

On a daily basis, read of God's greatness in Scripture. Remind yourself that God is both the creator of the world and the lover of your soul, and sit, humbled, in His presence. We don't need a telescope to see God. We just need open hearts, open eyes, and quieted spirits to dwell in His presence. We need to study His word, pray, and abide in Him—constantly reminding ourselves of who He is and who we are if we have surrendered our lives to Him. Old Testament history inspires a high and holy view of God as we see His mighty power on display, time and time again. The New Testament completes the story of His rescue plan, and then teaches us how to walk by faith. We must feed on truth—through the pages of Scripture, God-honoring books, sermons, and uplifting personal fellowship—so our soul's view of God remains in focus.

Psalm 34:8 says, "Oh, taste and see that the LORD is good! Blessed is the man who takes refuge in him!"

Unbuckle the first difficult strap by feasting on the holiness and majesty of God. And keep it unbuckled by making a commitment to daily (hourly!) dwell on His glory.

We must first bow down in reverent adoration of God, or we will be continually tempted to bow down to the lesser gods of culture and humanity.

If our hearts are bent in worship of the one true God, it will drastically alter our day-to-day living. Ask yourself through the day, as circumstances shift and challenges arise, "How does it make a difference that God is great, and that I am called to glorify Him—even in this?" When the house is a tornado of undone chores and upended toy bins, just as acquaintances are due to arrive for a meal. When the children squabble fierce and my nerves are frayed and hiding in the closet suddenly sounds appealing. When I fall short, and I am tempted to despair that I will never be good enough. When the phone rings, and the news is hard—even devastating. The way we respond to all of life depends on how we view God and how our hearts are aligned with His purposes.

This morning, I sat on the couch with four squirming girls and shared devotions with them. While Hope wiggle-wormed her way across our laps, Raina climbed over the armrest, and the older two kicked their feet in syncopated rhythm against the couch, I attempted to talk to my girls about the concept of having an undivided heart. It seemed ironic in light of our divided attentions! We read from Sally Michael's devotional, "To learn the fear of the Lord, you must have an undivided heart toward God. With all your heart you must be in awe of who God is, admire what He is like, and be amazed at His love."[28]

Our affections cannot be divided! I cannot extol God in one corridor of my soul, while simultaneously admiring money, fame, or power.

Psalm 86:11 says, "Teach me your way, O Lord, that I may walk in your truth; unite my heart to fear your name."

This verse shows us a clear truth about how we become undivided God-fearers. Did you catch it? The psalmist is praying, asking God to show him the way, how to walk in truth, and how to live sold-out, whole-hearted, all for Jesus.

We can't single-handedly manufacture a heartfelt, spirit-united, unwavering fear of the Lord. We need the help of the one we are called to fear! We need God to work in our hearts as we pray. We need to beseech Him for the ability to fear His name and walk daily in His perfect truth with hearts focused solely on His glory. Prayer is absolutely key. God is the one who works in us and enables us to live for Him. Without prayer, the fear of the Lord slides right back into the divided heart of man-pleasing.

In the last chapter, we talked about our spiritual identity as believers redeemed by the blood of Jesus. Obviously, we cannot begin to lay down the burden of pleasing man if we have not received the love and grace of Jesus

Christ. Our journey really begins the moment we open our hearts to receive the gift of salvation offered at the cross.

As we continue removing our proverbial backpacks, we need to believe we are truly made new in Christ! This morning, my wiggly four-year-old flibbertigibbet, precious Raina, started to throw an out-of-control temper tantrum over something small. She started to throw her little body onto the carpet, and just as she opened her mouth to scream, she tilted her chin, rolled over, and stopped herself. "Wait," she said. "Jesus gave me a new heart. I don't have to throw a fit." She looked me in the eyes, smiled, and said, "Okay, Mommy. I can do what you asked."

Of course, not all her childish struggles are fixed so easily! But she asked Jesus to forgive her sins, and she believes He has restored her to a right relationship with God. She believes she is born again, made new, and capable of turning away from sin because she has the Holy Spirit in her heart.

Do you believe that you are a new life in Christ? You are hidden in Him, covered by His blood, grafted into His family, and made lovely by His robes of perfect righteousness. Your sins and failures no longer define you. You are loved and you are beautiful because of Jesus' perfect sacrifice.

This is important! We will fail. Every day, I find myself recounting the ways I have fallen, struggled, and messed up. But Christ has covered each day's mess-ups with His shed blood, and when we fail, we have only to look to Him for a fresh outpouring of His kind mercy.

If we shoulder the weight of pleasing man, we will always look for approval and affirmation from those around us. We will never be satisfied, because each day will bring new failures, and we will stumble! Self-consciousness and pride will be the hallmark conditions of our hearts, depending on how we have (or have not) achieved the approval of others on a given day.

If we know Christ has remade us in Him, if we hold tight to the truth that we are His children and He loves us, we will love God above all else! We can live to please Him alone, and we can love others better as His Spirit works through us.

A right perspective of who we are in Christ is a double-sided truth. It enables us to see ourselves rightly, and it also corrects our view of others. If I live to please man, then relationships become a tool for building up my own self-esteem. I want others to think highly of me, and in relationship—even in service—I am preoccupied with their thoughts and approval. But if I am living for the glory of God, and if I understand all He has done for me, I also begin to think in a less self-focused manner about other people. I see them as beloved children of God, and I begin to care deeply about them, just as Christ does. Self-absorption gives way to genuine love. When I look with a lens fitted with the prescription of God's righteousness and love, I see people differently, and self-centeredness shifts to other-centeredness.

Philippians 2:1-4 says, "So if there is any encouragement in Christ, any comfort from love, any participation in the Spirit, any affection and sympathy, complete my joy by being of the same mind, having the same love, being in full accord and of one mind. Do nothing from selfish ambition or conceit, but in humility count others more significant than yourselves. Let each of you look not only to his own interests, but also to the interests of others."

Those verses are impossible to enact if we do not embrace a Christ-centered view of ourselves and of others.

I see this in my little ones, all the time. We tell them to "put the interest of other people first," and it is a sound admonition. It is the answer to so much of their petty bickering, and if they lived it out, it would transform our home! Our house would be a serene haven of like-minded, servant-hearted peacemakers! But they can't do it without surrendering to the Holy Spirit. They can't love each other selflessly unless they truly understand the gospel. I pray daily that the gospel would be great in their little lives—that they would understand and walk in the truth that Jesus loves them and died for them! But until He truly transforms their hearts, I expect this to be a daily struggle for my girls. Even regenerate hearts fumble with selfishness and pride! Our flesh is strong, and it will always be difficult to live without selfish ambition or vain conceit here on this sin-steeped earth.

Hebrews 11:6 tells us, "And without faith it is impossible to please him, for whoever would draw near to God must believe that he exists and that he rewards those who seek him."

But *with* faith, it *is* possible to please God. It is possible to "forget about ourselves and magnify the Lord and worship Him," as the old praise chorus goes.

One of the reasons we lust after man's approval is that we feel hollow inside. The rigors of earth drain our souls, and we feel needy, empty, and eager for the endorsement of other earthlings. We talked about this in chapter four, where we outlined a variety of false, felt needs and contrasted them with the real physical and spiritual needs God has placed within us.

Reach around your shoulder and find the buckle that controls the tautness of the strap. Lift the lever and let the strap slide through your fingers. Loosening this strap will require that we biblically evaluate our internal emptiness—our needs—and then replace our old, false expectations with the fullness of needs met in Christ.

Can Christ really meet our every need? Is He really the answer to every question?

Instead of reiterating the ways we wrongly place the weight of our happiness on how others respond to us, and the ways Christ's death and resurrection meet our deepest spiritual need for redemption, I want to focus on the names and attributes accorded to God in Scripture. When we see His many names and character-qualities, it is overwhelming. He can meet our every need because He is perfect in every way!

Philippians 4:19 says, "And my God will supply every need of yours according to his riches in glory in Christ Jesus."

Among other things, God is the Alpha and Omega—the beginning and end of all things. Revelation 1:8 says "'I am the Alpha and Omega,' says the Lord God, 'who is and who was and who is to come, the Almighty.'"

He is full of power. Jeremiah 32:17 says, "Ah, Lord God! It is you who have made the heavens and the earth by your great power and by your outstretched arm! Nothing is too hard for you."

He knows everything! 1 John 3:20 says, "For whenever our heart condemns us, God is greater than our heart, and he knows everything."

He is unchangeable. Numbers 23:19 says, "God is not man, that he should lie, or a son of man, that he should change his mind. Has he said, and will he not do it? Or has he spoken, and will he not fulfill it?" He keeps His promises.

He is a comforter, a mercy-giver. 2 Corinthians 1:3-4 tells us, "Blessed be the God and Father of our Lord Jesus Christ, the Father of mercies and God of all comfort, who comforts us in our affliction, so that we may be able to comfort those who are in any affliction, with the comfort with which we ourselves are comforted by God."

He grants us peace—a haven from life's swirling storms. Philippians 4:7 promises that if we surrender our anxieties and pray, "the peace of God, which surpasses all understanding, will guard your hearts and your minds in Christ Jesus."

He is our daily bread. John 6:48-51 says, "I am the bread of life. Your fathers ate manna in the wilderness, and they died. This is the bread that comes down from heaven, so that one may eat of it and not die. I am the living bread that came down from heaven. If anyone eats of this bread, he will live forever. And the bread that I will give for the life of the world is my flesh."

John 8:12 tells us He is the light of the world, "Again Jesus spoke to them, saying, 'I am the light of the world. Whoever follows me will not walk in darkness, but will have the light of life.'"

Isaiah 9:6 tells us that His name shall be called, "Wonderful Counselor, Mighty God, Everlasting Father, Prince of Peace."

He is the great shepherd (Hebrews 13:20).

He is the "same, yesterday, today and forever" (Hebrews 13:8).

He is our sufficiency. 2 Corinthians 3:5 says, "Not that we are sufficient in ourselves to claim anything as coming from us, but our sufficiency is from God."

Our big God is enough to meet our every need. And He chooses to dwell with us, to come low and walk with us, to call us His chosen people.

2 Corinthians 6:16 says, "I will make my dwelling among them and walk among them, and I will be their God and they will be my people."

We must loosen the tethers of our emotional neediness, and realize Jesus is sufficient to bear all of our valid needs.[29]

Does your load feel lighter yet? Let's keep going and tackle the other strap, now. As we settle into our new identity as believers, our trust in a mighty God, and our faith that He will graciously supply our every need, we must begin to look upward and outward instead of always focusing inward.

When we are wrapped in fear, insecurity, or self-consciousness, we are looking inward. We can be in a crowd, surrounded by people, with our thoughts focused narrowly on ourselves. We fret over mismatched socks (although my daughter Elisa frets if her socks are *not* mismatched), or frumpy hair, or misspoken words. We worry about whether we fit in. We fixate on what others might be thinking of us. Do they think I am dumb? Ugly? Do they think I am weird? We fidget, awkward and uncomfortable, because we are so concerned about ourselves!

I am an introvert. I draw strength from solitary moments, from prayer, reflection, and quiet. Too much activity or too many people render me restless and disjointed-feeling. I have to re-center, reenergize in the stillness. But I can't live life in the stillness, and I wouldn't want to. I must learn to function in the hustle and bustle, and I must learn to focus outward instead of always turning introspective and self-preoccupied.

You must, too. Even an extrovert can be self-focused—longing for attention, eager to be liked. Both the life of the party and the wallflower (yup, that's me!) can be inward focused in any relationship.

I think growing in this area is first a matter of abiding in prayer. It is a glance upward that says, "God, help me to glorify you in this relationship, in this setting, in this day, in this life. Help me not to seek my own honor, but to bring honor to you in all that I say and do."

And then it is prayer that extends outward, saying, "Lord, help me to love this person as you do. Help me to see her as you see her. Make me a blessing, and help me to be unconcerned with myself as I interact with her."

Earlier, I mentioned I struggle with large gatherings of women. My man-fearing flesh rears ugly, and I am so tempted to discouragement. For a long time, I have intentionally limited my exposure to those gatherings. As I have studied and prayed, though, I have decided to practice what the Lord has taught me by venturing out, just a little. Because of my season of life and commitment to my family, those opportunities are still few and far between. But, I am learning to face them with a renewed heart. Instead of shying away, I will go, and I will pray.

My prayers sound something like this.

"Lord, you know my struggles and temptations in this area! I am so prone to man-fearing in these situations, and I need you to protect my heart from discouragement. Help me, God, to focus my attention outward, rather than only thinking of myself, or of how others might perceive me. Help me to seek out those who are new, or lonely, or hurting. Help me to listen with an open heart, and help me to speak words of encouragement. Help me to dwell on You! Will you make me a conduit of your love to these women? Will you make me a blessing? Would you take away my awareness of self so I can focus on others? Help me to live out the gospel in every conversation."

The Lord has not miraculously cured me of my tendency to fear man. But I am learning to rely on His grace. If, mid-conversation, I begin to wrestle within my self-centered heart, I pray again. "God, help me!"

I am aware of my struggle, and I am learning to take that struggle to the throne of grace. Doesn't He promise to help us?

We must ask God to help us unbind the shackles of our fear of man—to help us care first and only about the glory of His holy name.

Prayer. Scripture. Worship. These three simple words are the crux of our undoing the hold man-fearing has on our hearts.

If Christianity has been woven into your story from infancy, you have probably lived through chapters of life when you took the Bible for granted. If we have been fed biblical truth for our entire lives, we might never have experienced a deep soul-hunger for it. Do you know what I mean? If the Lord saved you from a background void of His presence, then you probably feasted on His word—hungry to know all of His promises and devour the truth of who He is. For those of us raised on a steady diet of God-truth, it is easy to feel "full" and not recognize our need to be constantly and consistently feeding on His word. It usually takes some sort of about-face to make us identify the hunger within us to know God deeply and personally.

For me, that about-face came in college, when my beliefs were shaken by Christian professors who doubted the inerrancy of God's Word. I realized in a new way that I needed to study God's Word on my own! I needed to know Him personally, and I could only know Him by reading His love letter, over and over.

At that point, daily Bible reading became a mainstay for me. Seasons come and go, and there have been times when all I could muster was a quick perusal of a short devotional book, or a few verses. I have nursed babies all night, it seemed, sometimes, and during those weary months, the only Bible-reading I did was from a children's story Bible as I gathered little ones around and cradled a sleeping babe. Now, my little ones mostly sleep through the night, and the early morning is once again a sacred hour for seeking God.

If we want to have a vibrant, growing, world-changing walk with Lord, then studying His Word is non-negotiable.

Yesterday, I attended a Bible study at our church. The speaker shared about the time, shortly after she had rededicated her life to the Lord, when a woman had challenged her to wake up at 5:00 AM to read her Bible.

"Ha!" Deborah laughed. "What's option B?"

The friend smiled, but told her emphatically that there was no option B. Deborah's children were young and her days were full. Five o'clock in the morning was the only time where she could pray and study uninterrupted. So, she did it. And, she told us, after a few weeks of straggling from her bed in search of strong coffee, she began to rise joyfully, without even an alarm. God was calling to her heart, and she ran to His presence. Even at 5:00 in the morning.

There is no option B when it comes to studying God's Word. If we want to grow in the fear of the Lord, we must be steadfast in our commitment to learn about Him. Our souls need the nourishment of knowing God, of mediating on His word. If we are not filling our spirits with thoughts about God, then other thoughts creep in. And those thoughts don't nourish us. They deplete us. They turn us away from Him.

I have to admit, I don't get up quite so early. I wish I had the determined grit to pop up before the sun, but I struggle. I usually roll out of bed about 5:45, and am downstairs, clothed, combed, and scrubbed by 6:00. My earliest risers join me at 6:30, and if I am still studying or praying at that time, I ask them to choose a Bible from the nearby bin and read alongside me. Sometimes I make them a cup of tea to have with me, and they are content for a few minutes while I breathe my final prayers or jot down one last note.

I want to be clear that there is no biblical formula regarding our study of God's Word. My husband prefers to read his Bible in bed at night; I find I need to build my day on the steady foundation of an early morning quiet time. Different seasons and different personalities require different strategies, whether it is a stack of note cards you've printed verses on and keep nearby to thumb through, or an elaborate exegetical study complete with colored pencil drawings. And, while our study of God's Word is vital, we also need to approach our "time" with flexibility and grace. I know that I am sometimes tempted to guard my morning quiet too tightly. I can become disgruntled or annoyed if an alarm fails to sound or if a sweet little one needs her mama too early. That span of early morning serenity is not my time to claim; it is God's. We need to make meditating on Scripture a priority in our lives, and we also need to recognize that God is *with us* at every moment of the day. He is not limited to our quiet spaces.

We need to be in God's Word, and we need to pray. We can pray throughout the day—arrows shot up in each moment's desperation for God's help. We can come to God with our weakness, our immaturity, and our mess, and we can lay it all before Him, ask Him to pick up our pieces, and remake us in His image. But we also need to pray outward. Not just about the state of our own hearts, but about purposes and people outside of ourselves.

When I pray, I tend to journal for several minutes about the condition of my own spirit. I pray for patience as a mama, for wisdom, and for deep love to flow from my heart to those around me. I confess sins and ask God to cleanse my heart. And then, I slowly begin to pray for my husband, my children, and the needs of our family in general. I pray for growth in character, for strength to stand in truth, and for the joy of the Lord to fill their hearts. This takes time! By then, I hear footsteps pattering on floorboards, and I scurry to finish my prayers. Instead of praying intimately and specifically for the needs of those outside my immediate circle, I pray hurriedly in one breath for all them! "God, may your name be glorified throughout the world!" My prayer-time has been swallowed up by my inner "me monster!"

Dr. Welch suggests, "Try to pray backwards from the outer circle to the inner circle, by praying for the world and the church at large before getting closer to home."[30]

So, now, sometimes, when I pray, I do this. I pray the Word of God would spread to the ends of the earth, and I pray for missionaries on different continents who are faithfully sharing the gospel. I pray for natural disaster victims and for the hungry. I pray for orphans. I pray for friends, for extended family. And, then I pray for my kids. My husband. And on those days, when I pray "bigger," it is the me-prayers that get lost in the sounds of kids waking, in the busyness of oatmeal to be stirred and laundry to load.

There are still mornings when my heart is heavy, and I need to begin with the closest circle. I think that's okay. But praying in wider circles takes the heady, indulgent focus off our own needs, and teaches us to have other-focused hearts.

As we study and pray, let us not neglect to worship.

Can I share a story about my sweet little girl to illuminate the importance of worshipping the Lord? Yesterday, my Raina-bean did not want to nap. She is four, so naps no longer occur on a daily basis, but sometimes her constant motion catches up with her, and a nap becomes vital. Yesterday she was weary, out-of-control with sleeplessness. I tucked her in, but after thirty minutes, she pranced out and crept stealthily to the study area of my bedroom, where I was writing. I informed her nap time was not over, and my tired girl just lost it. She kicked and screamed and fought all the way back to her room. I was tempted for a moment to strictness, to give her a spanking (after all, she was still kicking me) and leave her in the room to scream herself to sleep. But the Lord showed me a different path. So, I scooped her up, stilled her flailing legs in my arms, and whispered words of love over her. I covered her with the quilt and ran my hand over her hair.

"Can Mama sing over you?" I asked. "Close your eyes." She obeyed, her eyes fluttering shut and her hair splaying ash-blonde over the green pillow. Sitting close, I stroked her cheeks and sang every praise chorus I could remember. Old ones, new ones. Sweet praise songs I remembered from college chapels and the fireside at Bible camp. I sang of God's goodness, of His love, of His great power. As I sang, the words of praise melted my Raina-girl into sound sleep. And, those same words filled up my heart. I tiptoed out of the room with my own soul bowed in worship. And for the rest of the day, those choruses stayed in my heart.

I forget to sing, sometimes. My house is noisy enough without music. But worshipping the Lord is such a beautiful way to focus on who He is, and it transforms our hearts as we sing boldly about what He has given to us.

Sing, my friends. Worship the Lord in song. You just might put your preschooler to sleep along the way!

How do we learn to live out the fear of God in our daily lives?

We obey Him. We study Scripture and let its truth permeate our lives, so our decisions, our passions, and our priorities become all about the gospel. We do the things He has commanded, and we rely on His Spirit to prepare a unique path for us in areas of freedom.

We love others. Empty cups filled up with all the mercy of Jesus, we pour out, loving people the way He does.

We serve. We plunge in, looking for ways to be the hands and feet of Jesus on His earth. We wipe runny little noses with soft hankies, offer bread and soup to friends and strangers, massage papery thin, wrinkled hands of great-grandmas with sweet lotion. We wash dishes, scrub toilets. We teach, and counsel, and listen. Maybe you run sound equipment in the back of the church sanctuary and no one notices until a microphone screeches loudly. Maybe you count the offering, fill the communion cups, vacuum pew crevices filled with broken crayons and bits of dusty Cheerios. Maybe you change diapers in the nursery, and hand babies back without hearing thanks. Maybe you travel, go to Africa, or India, and you wash the feet of the poor. Maybe God calls you there for a lifetime! Whatever we do, when we do it for the glory of our Lord, it is living out a right fear of Him. Give God your gifts, your talents, your limitations and weaknesses. Watch how He fills your time when you bend low, smile big, and open your hands to serve.

1 Peter 4:10 says, "As each one has received a special gift, employ it in serving one another as good stewards of the manifold grace of God."

For many years the motto of our local church has been "With all we are … loving God, and loving people through Christ." Simple. Yet, profound. We must first love God, fear Him, adore Him, trust in Him, and abide in Him. His love then flows through us, currents of mercy through our fingertips, and we love others. 1 John 4:19 says, "We love because he first loved us!"

That simple creed could be an outline for a God-fearing life. With all we are … our hearts undivided. We love God, and only in our reverent adoration for Him are we truly able to love mankind without succumbing to a misplaced fear of man.

Sometime around 30 A.D, a band of motley, discouraged disciples waited weary in Jerusalem, unsure of what the future held. Their beloved Master had been crucified on the hill, His body bloodied and broken before their very eyes. They wept for the loss of their friend, and for the loss of the hope they had placed on Him. He was gone.

But on Sunday morning, after the dark Sabbath day had passed, the women who loved Jesus went early to His tomb, taking spices and ointments to care for His body. When they went into the musty tomb, they found only a pile of empty linen cloths. A dazzling angel greeted them, asking, "Why do you seek the living among the dead? He is not here, but has risen" (Luke 24:6).

The women hurried to share the Good News with the disciples, but the words "seemed to them an idle tale, and they did not believe them" (v. 11). Peter rose and ran to the tomb; he saw the limp rags, the empty cavern. And he marveled.

Later that day, Jesus Himself appeared to two of His followers as they walked to a nearby village called Emmaus. He talked with them, discussed prophecy with them. Yet, it was not until the threesome sat at a table in Emmaus and He broke bread, blessing it, that they recognized Him.

Jesus had risen! Over the next forty days, He appeared to His followers. They saw His risen flesh, and their hope was renewed.

One day, Jesus led them "out as far as Bethany, and lifting up his hands he blessed them. While he blessed them, he parted from them and was carried up into heaven. And they worshiped him and returned to Jerusalem with great joy, and were continually in the temple blessing God" (verses 50-53).

Soon after Jesus' ascension into heaven, the disciples again gathered in the upper room. "And suddenly there came from heaven a sound like a mighty rushing wind, and it filled the entire house where they were sitting. And divided tongues as of fire appeared to them and rested on each one of them. And they were all filled with the Holy Spirit ..." (Acts 2:2-4).

Filled with the Holy Spirit, the disciples began to preach with new authority. They were bold and fearless, and they spoke truth clearly, passionately, and lovingly. They reached out to every faction of society with the gospel; they healed the sick; they performed signs and wonders.

Acts 2:42-45 gives a picture of the fellowship the believers shared as they lived out truth and the fear of God. "And they devoted themselves to the apostles' teaching and the fellowship, to the breaking of bread and the prayers. And awe came upon every soul, and many wonders and signs were being done through the apostles. And all who believed were together and had all things in common. And they were selling their possessions and belongings and distributing the proceeds to all, as any had need."

The disciples saw Jesus. They witnessed His life, His death, His resurrection, and His ascension. They experienced the all-at-once, rushing wind of the Holy Spirit descending to fill their hearts with His presence. They were filled, and they were awed. They feared the Lord, and, with hearts united in a single purpose, they lived for His glory. The fear of God changed them. In this unique fraction of Bible history, God allowed His power and might to be displayed through miracles and healings on a large and wondrous scale, calling people to Himself. Because of their love for God, they banded together, shared what they had, and lived in constant, loving fellowship with one another. They ate, they prayed, and they met the needs of the people around them as they proclaimed the message of the cross to all who would hear.

The Bible is chock-full of stories about people who feared God. Noah feared God when He built an ark on dry land and waited for storm waters to rise and lift it into rollicking waves. Moses feared God when He faced Pharaoh with his stuttering tongue and his shepherd's staff. Gideon feared God when he and his infantry of three hundred men sounded trumpets and smashed pottery loud, the echo sending Midianites fleeing in terror. David feared God when he faced off, small and weak, against Goliath, flattening the giant with a sling and a stone. The prophets feared God when they spoke truth the Israelites didn't want to hear.

But, I like the illustration given by the first Christ-followers. Some feared God even unto martyrdom, preaching the gospel with dying breaths. The story of the early church shows the progression of faith we are called to follow. They were awestruck by the Lord. They were filled with the Holy Spirit, and they became vessels for God to use for His glory. They loved, they served, and they built their entire lives on the gospel.

Times have changed, but our calling now is the same as it was then. We drop the backpack, we walk light, and we live a life of love.

CHAPTER EIGHT:

Portrait of the Unburdened Life

A light breeze rippled the blue-green surface of the lake, gentle waves lapping pebbles on the shore. I sat on wooden steps leading down to the boat launch, my littlest girl sound asleep in my arms. Bigger ones clambered up rocks wearing water shoes, ponytails flapping. Out on the water, our dented aluminum canoe floated, my husband's paddle carving neat, swift lines. On the step below me sat an old friend, a sweet mama whose husband had stood with mine on our wedding day. Our lives had intersected only briefly before Erik and I moved to another state, but she was still a woman I looked up to. Almost eight years later, her face still popped into my mind when I thought of godly womanhood. In fact, I had looked up to her so much during the early days of my marriage that I had feared her, been nervous around her. I was intimidated, awkward, and ill-at-ease because I knew I could never be as good a wife, as faithful a Christ-follower as she. Now, with our first babies reaching their middle elementary years, and the first twinges of gray fading our once dark hair (or at least mine), our families were together for a few days of fellowship and memory-making.

We sat there, cool wind kissing our cheeks, legs growing numb from the hard boards. Jebeke talked about the Lord, and the lessons He had been teaching her family over the years, lessons about faith, and about grace. "The gospel is so great in my heart now," she told me. And I could see that it was. In a beautiful way, she told me, God's grace had overcome a history of legalism and performance-based Christianity, and given her (and her husband) a new sense of wonder in the gospel. This petite mama had become a spiritual giant in the way she viewed God's grace, His sacrifice, and His love. The gospel was everything to her, and its truth seeped into every crack and crevice of her life. She had always been a wonderful, God-honoring woman. Her love for the Lord had always been evident in her speech and her conduct. But now, God has wowed her with His goodness in a new way, and it shows.

The gospel shows in the way she cares for her three children, with deep patience, Christ-like love, and gentle, biblical wisdom. It shows in the way she submits to her husband, with a quiet strength that is at once both tender and fiercely protective of his name and reputation. She is living out her calling as a wife and mother with a reverent fear of God and a genuine desire to make His name great. Her life proclaims the gospel, and it glorifies her God.

I still want to be like her, and I still wrestle with the feeling I will never be as good as my friend Jebeke. Now, however, I am choosing not to fear my friend. Rather, I want to pick up my walking stick, dump that old backpack by the wayside, and tromp along after her—following the path she's chosen, living a life that magnifies God and oozes gospel-truth at every turn.

What does it look like to live a life unburdened? How does an upward gaze and a right fear of God topple the idol of man-fearing in our hearts? How do the simplicity and awesome beauty of the gospel so penetrate our hearts that we are overcome with love for Christ and a desire to please Him, to serve Him, to honor Him?

Can you think of times in your life when you have encountered someone who was obviously free from self-concern? Someone who was blissfully unaware of herself (or himself) because she (he) was fixated on the Lord?

Before we think about the specific details of a gospel-centered life, I want to give you a few more caricatures. A few snapshots hidden in my memory bank offer a glimpse into the heart of a God-glorifier. So before we go any further, I want you to meet two more women and sketch from their stories a gentle outline of what it looks like to fear the Lord in the day to day.

Carly was a roommate of mine during college in Oregon. We only shared an apartment for a semester, and because she was busy with student teaching and I was deep in the throes of microbiology, our schedules rarely intersected. But I often passed Carly on the way home from a lab, climbing the steep stairs up from the campus "canyon," en route to the small prayer chapel on the edge of the quad. Her Bible, with its frilly cloth cover, would be tucked under her arm, and her clean, beautiful face would be radiant with the expectation of meeting in quiet with the Lover of her soul. During a season when most undergraduates were bent on pleasure-seeking, Carly stood out. She was a set-apart Christ-follower, and nothing could deter her from her heart's focus on living a gospel-saturated existence. You could not talk with Carly without her serene expression turning upward in a tender smile as she spoke the name of Jesus.

A few years later, in the spring of 2004, I was working as a pediatric nurse in Seattle, while planning a wedding for the coming winter. Carly had married her college sweetheart, and the Lord had brought them to a town just north of the city. Carly found my phone number, and invited me to share a meal with her and her husband at their home.

Eagerly, I accepted, and I drove north in my little white Oldsmobile. I was excited to see Carly and Nate, but I never imagined the impact that evening would have on my heart. The details of that simple dinner have stayed with me all these years, influencing my understanding of hospitality, friendship, and grace.

Because Carly and Nate were both just arriving home from work, the meal was prepped, but not cooked, when I arrived. Carly hugged me, eyes sparkling, and invited me into their tiny kitchen, where Nate began to simmer soup and bake bread that must have somehow been resting doughy in the refrigerator during the day. The kitchen filled with a tantalizing, spicy-sweet aroma as Carly led me around their cozy newlywed apartment.

Everything was natural, humble, unpretentious. There was no semblance of entertaining me; they just welcomed me with loving warmth to their home, and danced around me un-frazzled as they completed dinner with artful simplicity. The meal was delicious: a hearty soup, a fruit and nut-laced green salad, and dense, warm from the oven bread. Nate and Carly served me the first portion of each dish, and, as we ate, they focused kind attention on me, asking questions about my upcoming marriage, my work, and my walk with the Lord. I turned questions back to them, and, each answer came back to the evidences of God's mercy sprinkled throughout their lives.

As our soup bowls scraped clean and we lingered over bowls of vanilla ice cream and strawberries, Carly said, "We would love to pray for you."

I nodded, a little embarrassed.

Have you ever been prayed over? Really prayed over?

Carly lightly held my wrist across the table, and she poured out her heart to the Lord. In her prayer, she remembered each detail I had shared during dinner, praying for my career as a nurse and the specific long-term patients I had mentioned. She prayed for my relationship with God, and with Erik. She prayed for my wedding plans, and for our future marriage. She prayed for the children's ministry I helped with at my little church by Greenlake. She prayed for the missions trip I was preparing to go on in June.

Nate prayed, too. I remember that he prayed, specifically and with feeling, that Erik and I would stay strong in the area of physical purity as we waited for the wedding day. My cheeks tinged pink and I was thankful for the darkness of our closed eyes, but it struck me as so kind that this married man would remember what it was like to be engaged, and that he would pray for our purity, out-loud!

I felt full that night, as I drove home. Satiated by simple food lovingly prepared, and also full to overflowing with the gracious, Christ-honoring hospitality I had received. I was full spiritually, blessed by fervent, personal prayer.

I remember Carly filled old margarine tubs with leftovers and packed them in a brown paper bag for me to take for a workday lunch, so that the fullness flowed over into the next day!

Carly (and Nate) knew how to love people. They brimmed over with mercy, and the hospitality they offered was the most sincere, humble, and selfless hospitality I have ever experienced.

I have not seen Carly for many years, now. But I am certain she still loves people with the same focused attention and God-ward gaze as she did on that memorable evening. She loves God, and is conscious only of Him. She cares deeply about others, because she sees them as people who are loved deeply by her God. She fears God and she loves people. Simply.

The next portrait is of a woman named Sera.

For seven years, my husband and I have rented the home I grew up in, a large, two-story ranch home in Wyoming. There is a barn on the same property—though it is a barn in name only. It has a comfortable two-bedroom apartment in what was once the barn loft, and in the time we have lived here, three wonderful couples have shared land with us, across the pond.

Matt and Sera were the second couple. When they moved in, their oldest son was an infant, and I was busy chasing an almost three year old and a crawler. For three and a half years, our feet wore a trail across the land bridge that cuts between marsh and pond. Sera and I shared life and a backyard, our bellies burgeoning big with new babies. Sera's belly, I might add, burgeoned somewhat larger than mine, as her womb held not one, but two baby girls.

We never seemed to plan our get-togethers; instead, the girls and I would dash over to drop off a package that had been left on the wrong doorstep, and we would stay for two hours. Or, we would meet spontaneously at the swings in the yard, and then gather ingredients for a shared picnic on the lawn. We saw each other's children throw fits and swing fists. We talked about good books, and the Bible, and how to live ordered, disciplined, and intentional lives with our busy, wonderful little people. We laughed about the things they did, and the things we said in response. We talked about our sin, and our kids' sin, and how much all of us needed a Savior. I don't know if Sera was as encouraged by our times together as I was, but her sweet countenance and gentle wisdom left an indelible mark on my life.

And here is the reason why.

Everything Sera did was informed by the gospel. Every decision she made, every word she spoke, every teaching moment with her children … from the way she structured her housework, to the way she taught her kids Scripture, to the way she attended to her husband's needs … all of it was filtered through the truth of God's grace.

Once, we sat by the pond, little ones tossing rocks into the water, our new babies in arms or sleeping in nearby strollers. As we watched the rings of water and reminded our sweet ones repeatedly to watch out for one another as they threw their rocks, we talked about the early weeks of life with her twins. Both girls were fussy, and their schedules were hard to match. Nursing was a challenge, and she found nursing both babies at once to be impossible. I knew she had to be bone-tired from the strain of caring for two newborns and a little boy who was not yet eighteen months old. I was weary from the constant demands of my own baby girl, and I only had one infant!

She told me that, yes, it was difficult. But her love for the Lord compelled her to stay the course, to nurse her babies—even though formula might have made feeding times simpler and given her body more rest. She said, "Jesus suffered the cross for me. By His grace, I can do this for my babies." She wasn't making a judgment about feeding choices; she was saying the gospel was so great to her that the temporary trials of here and now seemed small. She knew, too, that His grace was sufficient to sustain her, body and spirit, through the sleepless nights and overwhelming tiredness of her season.

At other times, we talked about training our kids up in the Lord, and I would leave impassioned about amazing my girls with the depth of Jesus' love for them. The gospel was a part of every disciplinary moment for Sera, grace poured out for that child's sin. We talked about the nitty-gritty details of managing our homes: the meal-planning, the cleaning, the laundry, and the never-ending upkeep of toy bins and bookshelves. We talked about education, and the importance of reading to our children. We passed books back and forth.

Sera, Matt, and their four children (they added another baby girl shortly before their twins' third birthday) now live across town. I don't see her very often these days. But I still drink often from the well of wisdom she left behind. I think of how intentionally she lived (and still lives!) each day, choices all undergirded by thought, prayer, carefully sought counsel, and a netting of gospel grace.

None of the three women I've shared about are spectacular by the world's standards. They are not history-makers. They are homemakers, mamas, and wives—everyday women who clean bathrooms in sweatpants and stir soup pots while toddlers bang on lids at their feet. But can you glimpse in each short story the common thread?

Jebeke, Carly, and Sera all fear the Lord. Their lives are not ordered to bring glory to themselves, or to earn the appreciation of other people. Their lives are structured with Biblical priorities, and on the top rung is the fame and renown of their Savior, Jesus Christ. Everything they do points to His grace. Their lives and hearts are full of the good news, and it has transformed them!

Can you picture someone in your life who embodies a similar heart for the Lord? Someone whose heart has swelled large with the greatness of the gospel? Someone who doesn't seek recognition or accolades, but serves with the upward focus of seeing God praised and truth spread?

I picked examples of ordinary women to share with you because I think we can be God-fearers in our homes, in our churches, and in the mundane details of our quiet, run of the mill daily lives. We don't have to do crazy, brave things and demonstrate our fear of God by fighting giants with slingshots or standing bold before kings to plead for the protection of our nation (Remember Esther? She did that. She feared God enough to risk her life for the sake of Israel).

We can follow God to do seemingly crazy, wildly brave things, though. You never know where the fear of the Lord might lead you! A beautiful, God-fearing widow in our church felt the Lord was calling her back to the region of Kenya where she and her husband had served as missionaries before he died of cancer. So she went, in her mid-seventies. It seemed crazy. But she feared the Lord more than she feared the opinions of the naysayers. She has now gone back several times, each time for a length of three to six months. Once she took with her a team of eighteen ladies from our community. She teaches Bible classes, ministers to women, plays with children, and walks steep hills every day to the church and school where she serves. Oh, how I want to grow up to be like Rozan!

My girls and I love to read missionary biographies. Immersing ourselves in the fearless lives of historical missionaries gives a great picture of what the Lord can do with lives surrendered to Him. We loved reading about George Mueller, who, by faith and prayer, started a group of orphanages in Bristol, England. Others scoffed when he shared the magnitude of what he hoped to accomplish, but he feared God and he trusted God would provide for the needs of the many homeless children. He watched miracle after mir-acle transpire.

A biography of Gladys Aylward is waiting on my shelf right now, and I can't wait to crack the cover with my girls and see how God was glorified in her gospel-centered ministry in China.

There are so many stories—biblical, historical, and modern—about how God has used ordinary people to do great things, simply because they feared Him, loved Him, and trusted Him.

I don't know the Lord's plans for your life, and I don't know His plans for mine. Remember when we talked about how the path He is laying for each of us is different? Living a life that reveres God is not necessarily about the particulars of our career choices, or where we decide to live, or the ways He equips us to serve. It's about our hearts. It's about firm faith, relentless trust, and open hands. It's about receiving the gifts He hands us with grati-tude, unfurling the death grips we have on our own lives, and surrendering control to Him. It's about tilting our empty cups up, and watching Him pour love into our lives—love that spills messy through the cracks and overflows onto the people around us. It's about being molded and shaped by His hand so we can be used for His service, to His glory. It's about learning to see with His eyes.

Ephesians 2:10 says, "For we are his workmanship, created in Christ Jesus for good works, which God prepared beforehand, that we should walk in them."

In a recent sermon, my pastor shared that the Greek word for work-manship is *poiema,* the same word from which the English word "poem" is derived. Scholars don't all agree on the best translation for the word, but the definition seems to go beyond the brick and mortar of "workmanship." We are God's masterpiece, His poem. With graceful strokes of His brilliant art-istry, He is rendering something beautiful out of the scraps and shards of His people. We were created by Him, to do the works He prepared beforehand for us to accomplish.

Do you love the thought that God is writing poetry with us? We are the lyrical lines of truth He is penning to the world. He is using our lives to author the poem of His glory!

Sometimes I don't feel like a poem. I feel a bit like the messy, scrawled out mistakes in the margins of the rough draft. I am ink scratched out, blotted.

But God calls us his *poiema*, and He has jobs for us to do. Masterpieces for us to create.

Part of our new, lightened journey as God-fearers (as opposed to our heavy-laden trek as man-fearers) is discovering the unique work He has prepared for us. What is the "poem" our lives are intended to write?

We each have gifts. Sometimes, in my ink-blot moments of personal discouragement, I wonder why everyone else seems to have so many talents, and I am inept in so many areas. But God does not distribute cookie-cutter aptitudes to His followers. He crafts our gifting as uniquely as He writes our genetic code. When I fix my eyes on Jesus, and take my gaze off my own failings, He works through me to splash beauty and joy onto the pages of my story—and into the world around me.

You know when it happens. When you're serving out of fullness, when you're doing what you were made to do, when you're being paint spattered bright on the masterpiece of His making. I feel it when I dig deep, dive in, and love my children well, when I play Legos, stack blocks, talk in British accents, and laugh! I feel it when my four girls snuggle close and we—all of us—read stacks of library books together, time falling away. I feel it when I pray, gripping my daughters' hands at the curb of their new school. I feel it when I make my husband's favorite meal, serve it on our wedding china, and surprise him with dessert. I feel it when I teach in the basement of our church, children seated on carpet squares, wiggly legs crossed to listen. And

I feel it when I write, when I take thoughts, gather them in bunches, and tie ribbons to make a pretty bouquet of words! Those things are what I was created to do! To make bread in my sunlit kitchen, and laugh as little blonde girls overfill the cookie dough with chocolate chips. To fold laundry, thankful for so many pairs of little pink socks and frilly mounds of dresses. I was made to love and serve God out of my unique personality, the workmanship a natural extension of my heart's bent towards home and hearth and story.

How is your heart bent? How does God want to use you, unburdened, to serve Him?

I pose the question to my girls some mornings when I rouse them from slumber. "How do you think God wants to use you today, Sadie?" I ask my six-year-old. "What part do you have in His story?" What poem does He want to write with you? I bring it up again at bedtime, as we pray. "God has plans for your life. I pray you will live surrendered to Him, let Him work through you. I wonder how He wants to use you for His glory."

I wonder, often, what God will do with their little lives.

Sadie, my Sadie. My second child. She is beautiful, all long blonde hair (though she just cut her own bangs before the first week of school) and big brown eyes that twinkle bright when she smiles her happy-go-lucky grin. She is laughter and sweetness, and she talked in sentences at eighteen months. She still chatters and tells stories with detail and animation. She is a brave adventurer and an outgoing friend. She is loyal. She's silly, and a little flighty, and she just makes me giggle—even when I have to tell her eight times to put her shoes on. She loves Jesus and reading the Bible. And she notices everything!

What masterpiece will God make of Sadie's precious life? Where will she go? What will she do? What will be her spiritual gifts, her artistry, her poem? Erik and I wonder if she will be our missionary—our bold explorer venturing to places unknown to love people she's never met. But we don't know. I do know God has something prepared for her, and that as she grows in the fear of the Lord, He will faithfully make her path straight!

What will God do with Elisa's strong spirit, love of beauty, determination, and sense of justice? What will He do with Raina's unstoppable energy, laser focus, and tender heart? And my baby-my Hope-girl—what about her? What art, what masterpiece, is waiting on the fresh canvases of their lives?

My husband figured out early what he was wired to do. As a boy, tinkering and taking apart and putting back together, he decided God had made him to be an engineer. And, while he would grimace at calling engineering "art," he is in his artistic element when he is planning, ciphering, and creating. When Erik designs, builds, and perfects as a civil engineer, he is doing the work God has prepared for him to do. He's suited for it; he enjoys it. It's not the only work God has called him to; he is a natural leader, a talented teacher, and an avid outdoorsmen. In all of those things, he is fulfilling the roles and callings God has given him.

My mama was widowed seven years ago. She had poured her heart into the work of raising her four children and being a helpmate to her husband of thirty-four years. After my dad's death, though, the Lord breathed life into a dormant seed of artistic skill within her fingertips. She decided to become certified in floral design, and discovered a talent for creating intricate, unique flower arrangements. She blesses brides, comforts the grieving, and brings a touch of beauty wherever she goes.

We take the gifts God has planted within us, and we abide in Him, branches of the vine, and He bears fruit in us!

When we fear God, our lives bloom—petals opening soft in spring.

Today, I padded in stocking-feet across the driveway to bring back the garbage can. Pebbles poked the soles of my feet, and suddenly it was raining, drizzling wet from an autumn blue sky. I danced giddy at the miracle of fall rain, and the hillside alight with yellows and oranges splattering what was green only a few days ago. The world looked like an oil painting, with dabs of thick color smudged onto the brown earth. Inside, I made quiche for dinner, swirling yellow egg yolks through white cream in the bowl, and stirred in cheese and diced ham, then filled a pie plate with the mixture. Laundry hummed as it spun through the washer. I checked on napping girls upstairs, and listened to their steady breathing. I squeezed dish soap into warm water and scrubbed the bowl.

When I fear God and I recognize that these simple moments are a part of the workmanship He is making of my life, I experience joy. The mundane becomes miraculous because I am doing it all for Him, and not for any earthly glory.

Maybe it seems too simple, but living the unburdened life is, in part, about leaning into the way we are made, and living out our faith through our unique temperaments. Remember back in chapter four, when we talked about how self-esteem is a fallacy and we can't manufacture confidence simply by embracing our inner beauty? That's true! We are not called to just be ourselves! Rather, we are called to be who we are *in Christ*. It's a subtle difference, yes, but I think it's also vital. As we fear God and walk light in His grace, we become who we were made to be, and we do what we were made to do. And, perhaps most importantly, the things we do flow out of the right, God-centered motivations.

I don't wash dishes and mop floors because I want my home to be prepared for unexpected company who might judge my homemaking skills and find them lacking (or at least I pray that is not my motivation!). I care for my home because when it is orderly, it is welcoming. It is a haven for my family, friends, and visitors. I do the same things, the same old chores that beg repeating on a daily basis. On one hand, I do them under compulsion, because I want to be thought highly of, and it leads to stress. On the other hand, I do them out of love, because I want to serve, and it brings freedom. If the toys are scattered and there are dishes in the sink, it does not make my home unwelcoming. But if I am so fretful about those toys and dishes that I grow stressed and irritable in the tasks of cleaning them up, then my *heart* becomes unwelcoming. I am fearing people, instead of loving people.

Are those differences resonating in your spirit? Are you catching a glimpse of how the rhythms of everyday life might unfold gracefully from a heart bowed to God and not man?

Let's keep going.

When I was young, I thought that becoming an adult meant becoming perfect. I thought I would blow out candles on my thirtieth birthday cake and I would suddenly have life figured out. My frizzy brownish hair would suddenly straighten and turn blonde. My acne-prone skin would magically smooth to porcelain clarity. I would have white teeth, confident speech, and I would never need an alarm clock because I would bound from bed at six o'clock every morning! I would never struggle with sin, with pettiness, with frailty.

You know what though? I am a few years past thirty, now. And, I'm not perfect. My hair is still reckless and untamable. I still fight shy awkwardness. I still hit snooze at least once in the morning. And, I still sin. Every single day.

How does a God-fearer respond to the reality that sin is still a part of our earthly lives? We know how a man-fearer responds. With shame. With hiding. With despair. We bury, we whitewash, we cover-up, and we hang our heads.

But that backpack is by the wayside now. So, fearing the Lord, we respond to sin differently. We confess our wrongdoing to the Lord in prayer, and we give it to Him, knowing He has paid the price for it. In Psalm 103:12, we read, "as far as the east is from the west, so far does he remove our transgressions from us." He has redeemed us from the bondage of that sin!

When we lose sight of our position as saints, we succumb so easily to the fear of man—to feeling we are letting others down, that they don't approve of us, or are disappointed in us. But we have the record of Christ, and those mishaps that mark our lives are just means of moving us closer to Him as we see our deep need of a Savior.

When we sin and we stand messy and broken before God, He is faithful to forgive us. He is also faithful to strengthen our spirits so that by His grace, we can conquer the patterns of sin in our lives. I have heard it said that God loves us while we are still sinners, but He loves us too much to let us stay that way! He wants to equip us to glorify Him with holy, honorable, and righteous lives.

When we fear God, we want to obey Him! And though we fail, we always come back to the Word, seeking ways to obey Him more fully, to live up to the record we have attained in Christ.

I John 3:9 says, "No one born of God makes a practice of sinning, for God's seed abides in him, and he cannot keep on sinning because he has been born of God."

As God-fearers, we continue to mess up. So we take those mess-ups, we give them over to the Lord, and we ask Him to help us learn from our mistakes. Our sins are not wasted if they lead us to the foot of the cross.

A woman (or a man) who fears the Lord bases decisions on biblical truth, godly counsel, and the leading of the Holy Spirit. She is not swayed by popular opinion, the desire for approval, or an aspiration to fit in with a certain group. God-fearers are free to walk by faith, to trust God for each step, even in the foggy unknown. They don't have to follow extra-biblical or secular formulas for daily living.

As God-fearers follow the Lord along the path of life, their mouths are filled with praise of the One who made and loves them. They worship God from the heart, seeking only His pleasure, and concerned only about living so His name is honored.

God-fearers love others from the wellspring of God's love within their over-filled, redeemed hearts! They don't worry about reciprocation, because the love they offer is given as an imitation of the love God has given them. They don't love others because they need to be loved in return; they love because they are image-bearers of the living God, and God is love!

God-fearers give generously, share the gospel boldly, and meet the needs around them with mercy and compassion.

I don't yet count myself among the ranks of those who have abandoned the fear of man completely and are living solely for the glory of God. But, I long to be a God-fearer. Don't you?

I saved my favorite biblical portrait for last, and I hope you will savor this tender story with me as we close. It's the story of two faithful women, two mamas, who faithfully walked the paths set before them.

Elizabeth was the wife of Zechariah, who served as a priest in Judah. Luke tells us that Elizabeth and Zechariah "were both righteous before God, walking blamelessly in all the commandments and statutes of the Lord. But they had no child, because Elizabeth was barren, and both were advanced in years" (Luke 1:6-7).

One day, Zechariah was chosen by lot to enter the temple and burn incense, a high honor among the many priests who served in his division. As he worshiped in the temple, the others gathered outside to pray. While Zechariah burned the incense, the angel Gabriel appeared to him and said, "Do not be afraid, Zechariah, for your prayer has been heard, and your wife

Elizabeth will bear you a son, and you shall call his name John. And you will have joy and gladness, and many will rejoice at his birth, for he will be great before the Lord" (v 13-15). The angel foretold that John would be filled with the Holy Spirit, that he would go before the Messiah in the spirit and power of Elijah, and that he would turn the hearts of the children of Israel to the Lord. Zechariah scoffed a little, bewildered by what had been foretold. Because of his doubt, Zechariah was struck mute for the duration of the baby's gestation.

Elizabeth conceived; miracle birthed in her once-closed womb.

Six months later in Galilee, Elizabeth's young relative, a girl named Mary, was visited by Gabriel (the same angel who had spoken to Zechariah). He promised Mary the Holy One would overshadow her, fill her virgin womb with the very Son of God. She would conceive and give birth to Jesus, the Messiah, God's own Son. Gabriel told Mary that Elizabeth, her barren relative, was also with child. "For nothing is impossible with God," he said (Luke 1:37). Humbly, Mary bowed in acquiescence to God's plan. "Behold, I am the servant of the Lord," she said (verse 38).

Mary went with haste to Judah and she entered Elizabeth's home. And here is the part where I shiver with wonder. Elizabeth was filled with the Holy Spirit and with a breath of startled gratefulness, she exclaimed, "Blessed are you among women, and blessed in the fruit of your womb! And why is this granted to me that the mother of my Lord should come to me? For behold, when the sound of your greeting came to my ears, the baby in my womb leaped for joy. And blessed is she who believed that there would be a fulfillment of what was spoken to her from the Lord" (verses 42-45).

Mary was barely pregnant. There was nothing about her physical appearance to give away the truth that God's seed grew within her. The Spirit gifted Elizabeth with a clear revelation, and she knew what the Lord had done for Mary and what He was doing for the world through her!

Mary responded with the famous song of praise known as the *Magnificat*:

> *And Mary said, "My soul magnifies the Lord, and my spirit rejoices in God my Savior, for he has looked on the humble estate of his servant. For behold, from now on all generations will call me blessed; for he who is mighty has done great things for me, and holy is his name. And his mercy is for those who fear him from generation to generation. He has shown strength with his arm; he has scattered the proud in the thoughts of their hearts; he has brought down the mighty from their thrones and exalted those of humble estate; he has filled the hungry with good things, and the rich he has sent away empty. He has helped his servant Israel, in remembrance of his mercy, as he spoke to our fathers, to Abraham and to his offspring forever" (verses 46-55).*

Can you picture the sweet joy of these two women, each with their own path to walk, each surrendered to the will of God, each worshipping the Lord out of the fullness of their God-fearing hearts? Can you imagine the tenderness of their fellowship, their shared awe at how the Lord had chosen them to bring His redemption story to completion? It wasn't easy. The roads they travelled were difficult, filled with heartache. The babies they carried were destined to do the will of the Father, even unto death. But these sweet women, one old, one young, both feared the Lord and they held their heads high even as their spirits were bowed low in worship. Mary suffered persecution, misunderstanding. She was perceived as an unwed mother and she no doubt experienced the sting of rejection. But she didn't fear the approval of others in Nazareth. She feared God, and she trusted Him to lead her. Elizabeth firmly pronounced her newborn baby's name as "John," even when well-meaning attendants pressured her to name him after his father. When

Zechariah agreed with her choice, his mouth was opened, and he, too, spoke words of praise to God.

Scripture doesn't give us any reason to think that Mary or Elizabeth were spectacular by the world's standards, either. They were gentle-spirited and quiet Jewish women, hard-working, simple, and unremarkable. They loved the Lord, and when He called, they were willing to serve Him. They were like clay, fashioned by the skilled hands of the Potter, and set apart as sacred vessels for His purposes. The fear of the Lord transformed them, and it allowed them to be used!

A few months ago, we went on a hike as a family above an alpine lake. We started innocently up the trail, but soon my husband gestured for us to shift off the trail and veer up the steep mountainside instead. I looked at him a little quizzically. "What's wrong with seeing where the trail leads?" I asked.

"See that ridge?" He pointed. "I think we can make it up there if we just go straight up. Are you game?"

Erik doesn't like trails. He wants to explore the unknown—not amble safely down the beaten path. Me? I'm a bit more of a steady-footing, even trail kind-of-girl. But, I trust my husband. Whole-heartedly. Experience has taught me he has good judgment, and that he will never take us somewhere he can't help us get through. He has confidence, skill, a keen sense of direction, and hearty legs and hands to guide us (or carry us) through any adventure. I am willing to go anywhere he leads, because I trust him, and if he is with me, I know I can make it. And so can our girls.

So, I looked up at the crumbling stone hillside and turned to him with a shrug, and a smile. "You know I kind of like trails, honey. But I'm willing to follow you."

So we embarked straight up the hill. Hope napped on my back as I labored one foot at a time up the hill, and Erik gripped our older daughters' hands to help them over steep and slippery sections. We stepped gingerly through briars, groped our way through tall bushes, and clambered up rock-strewn mountain faces. We gaped wide-eyed at rock formations, wondering at color, shape, and geology. We took turns charting the course, girls trotting brave as they led the way. We stood high up and gazed down at the lake, marveling at the green-blue of the water, and the clear delineations of an old landslide. We sang, and we laughed. We snacked on trail mix, and enjoyed the beauty all around us. Beauty we might have missed if we had just stayed passively on the well-worn trail.

I think walking in faith with the Lord looks a little like hiking with my husband. The trail is not always clearly marked. But we can trust our God! He wants to lead us to beautiful places and sometimes that means we have to hold tight to His strong hand as He guides us up mountain sides and along crumbling rock scarps. No, we probably couldn't find the way all on our own. We need our trail guide, the Holy Spirit. God has promised to prepare a way for us, and it might be a steep, winding path that seems difficult and little travelled. But He is with us—and He is trustworthy.

Let's leave our backpacks behind so we can follow God unhindered. His burden is lighter than the one we are so tempted to pick up. Let's grab hold of His strong and mighty hand and run with Him, finding joy in His presence. Let's bring glory to His name and not chase after glory for ourselves.

My prayer is that you and I would abandon the weight of man-fearing and that, together, we would fear the Lord alone.

When we meet in the grocery store aisle, or the church foyer, I pray that we would love one another better because we have learned to love Him first. I pray we would wash each other's feet—and maybe even scrub each other's toilets—because we have learned to serve and not to show off. I pray we would see the Lord in one another and that together, we would make His gospel known to the world.

Shake off those old hindrances, my friend, and walk light in His grace!

AFTERWORD

Bare trees limbs are whipping hard outside my window, driven by a warm spring wind. Soon, buds will appear on the aspens and willows, as melting snow and days of sunshine weave their April magic. I am reminded that I have sat here, in the study nook off my bedroom, through the changing of several seasons, learning and writing about the topic of fearing God, and not man. Some things in my life have changed since I began the journey of writing this book. My belly is rounded now with a baby whose life was not even a spark in our thoughts when I began the writing process. We finally replaced the scratched white dining table I wrote about several times with a long wooden farmhouse table and benches. My older girls are now nearing the end of their first year of "real" school, and we find ourselves again in decision-making mode. Seasons pass and life brings changes—some important, and some insignificant (like the color of my dining table). But, for all the ways, big and small, that life looks different today than it did a year ago, I still struggle with a sinful tendency to exalt the applause of man over the pleasure of my God.

A few weeks ago, I was lamenting to my husband that my schedule for the next day included a dental check-up. I hate going to the dentist. My husband asked me why it was such a big deal, and I responded, "Because the hygienist will clean my teeth, and she will judge me! She'll find stains and plaque, and she'll know that I am not perfect at brushing and flossing my teeth!" Erik laughed at me, and then replied seriously, "Honey, didn't you write a book about that?" He was right, of course. Unfortunately, it's a daily battle to keep my heart and mind focused on God's glory, instead of focusing on the approval of those around me.

Maybe someday that, too, will change. I know that in Heaven my eyes and my thoughts will be ever fixed on Christ. Until then, though, I expect to have to fight to live an unburdened life. And so will you. Our human, sinful tendency is to seek glory for ourselves, to be self-focused, people-pleasing man-fearers.

The teaching I laid out in the last eight chapters is not a one-time cure. To live for the glory of God, to shed the fear of man and walk light, requires us to choose, every single day, whom we will serve.

Today, and tomorrow, and the next day, as the seasons circle again and life blooms with change, I want to choose Christ.

And I pray you do, too! If you would like to dive deeper into this book as you seek to pursue the unburdened life, please join me at www.messes-and-miracles.blogspot.com to download your free study guide. I pray that working through this book and the accompanying questions kick-starts your journey to finding freedom and joy in Christ alone.

ACKNOWLEDGMENTS

I am deeply indebted to several people whom I have never met for spurring me on as I wrote this book. The Lord nudged me to pick up my pen and write again through the poignant writing of Emily P. Freeman. And, when He touched my heart with a very specific topic, He also led me to a wonderful biblical counseling book by Dr. Edward Welch. His perspective was just what I needed as I sought to define the fear of man. The writings of Leslie Ludy informed and encouraged me, as did the work of Angie Smith. Elyse Fitzpatrick offered solid, scriptural counsel when I needed clear definitions for some of those weighty topics. I am grateful for how the Lord has used those authors to proclaim His gospel and to equip believers to walk faithfully.

I am also grateful for the help of friends! Pastor Ray McDaniel took time to read my work and give feedback. His wife, Tanya, painted the cover for me. Thank you for lending your amazing talent to make my book beautiful! Jebeke Adams read the book from cover to cover, finding herself unexpectedly featured in the last chapter. Her insights were both gracious and helpful. Amy Litzelman met with me over tea to share her insights on publishing, and Sandy Landis helped with the final editing. My mama and two sisters (Amy and Michelle) also read early drafts and encouraged me to keep going. I am so grateful for each of you!

My husband put up with the bluish glare of the computer screen interrupting his sleep on many early mornings or late nights as I wrote. He also read the entire manuscript sitting in an airport terminal between flights and offered tender encouragement. I am so thankful for his constant, steady, and loving support. I am so glad that I said "I do!" I love you now. I will love you forever. You are the love of my life.

My wonderful kiddos woke up from many naps to find Mommy tapping away at the computer, and they were gracious to give me "just five more minutes to finish this paragraph!" I love you so much, girls! This book is dedicated to you, because the desire of my heart is that you would bravely, with unfettered devotion, follow the Lord wherever He leads you. May you live unburdened for His glory.

And, gracious Father, you are so kind to me! Thank you for making the gospel dearer, Your Word more real and active, and your Spirit's work in my heart even gentler as I wrote this book. I pray it brings others closer to You!

ABOUT THE AUTHOR

Colleen Wachob is a follower of Jesus, a wife who is deeply in love with her husband, and a stay-at-home mama of five children. She graduated from the University of Washington with a degree in nursing, but now mostly uses her medical training to pull out slivers, bathe fevered brows, and apply bandages to little-girl scrapes. You can find her blogging (but only sporadically) at www.messes-and-miracles.blogspot.com. More often, you can find her exploring the Wyoming wilderness with her adventurous family, curled up with a stack of picture books and her sweet daughters, or teaching Bible stories to wiggly preschoolers in the church basement.

NOTES

[1] W.L. Walker. "Fear." *International Standard Bible Encyclopedia*. n.p. n.d. Web. Accessed April 30, 2014. http://www.blueletterbible.org/search/Dictionary/viewTopic.cfm?topic=IT0003396

[2] Lewis, C.S., *The Lion, the Witch, and the Wardrobe* (London: Geoffrey Blessing, 1950)

[3] Edward T. Welch, *When People Are Big and God Is Small* (Phillipsburg, NJ: P&R Publishing, 1997), 98

[4] Ibid, 71.

[5] Sally Lloyd-Jones, *The Jesus Story Book Bible* (Grand Rapids, MI: Zondervan, 2007), 348.

[6] Welch, *When People are Big and God Is Small, 24.*

[7] Ibid.

[8] Angie Smith, *What Women Fear: Walking in Faith that Transforms* (Nashville, TN: B&H Publishers, 2011), 55.

[9] Elyse M. Fitzpatrick, *Found in Him: the Joy of the Incarnation and Our Union with Christ* (Wheaton IL: Crossway Books, 2013), 184.

[10] Ibid., 185.

[11] Emily P. Freeman, *A Million Little Ways: Uncover the Art You Were Made to Live* (Grand Rapids, MI: Fleming H. Revell, 2013), 83

[12] John Piper, "Glorifying God ... Period." July 14, 2013. Web. Accessed May 2014. http://www.desiringgod.org/conference-messages/glorifying-god-period

[13] Freeman, *A Million Little Ways: Uncover the Art You were Made to Live,* 199-200

[14] Ibid., 200.

[15] Elyse Fitzpatrick, *Idols of the Heart: Learning to Long for God Alone* (Phillipsburg, NJ: P&R Publishing, 2001), 14.

[16] Ibid., 138.

[17] Welch, *When People Are Big and God Is Small,* 9.

[18] My thoughts on this topic were influenced by Ed Welch's book, *When People Are Big and God Is Small.* For a more thorough treatment of these topics, please see *Chapter 9 – Know Your Real Needs.*

[19] Leslie Ludy, *Set-Apart Femininity* (Eugene, OR: Harvest House Publishers, 2008), 46.

[20] Leslie Ludy has written a wonderful chapter in her book, *Set-Apart Femininity,* which greatly informed my thinking on this issue. Please see *Chapter Two, Sacred Design.*

[21] Sally Michael, *God's Wisdom* (Phillipsburg, NJ: P&R Publishing, 2014), 69.

[22] Ibid., 70.

[23] Ibid., 74.

[24] Wayne Grudem, *Bible Doctrine: Essential Teachings of the Christian Faith* (Grand Rapids, MI: Zondervan, 1999), 92.

[25] Stuart Townend, "How Deep the Father's Love for Us," Thankyou Music, 1995

[26] Johnny Mac Powell, Bradley B. C. Avery, Mark D. Lee, David Carr, Samuel Tai Anderson, "King of Glory"
New Spring Publishing Inc., 2000.

[27] *The MacArthur Study Bible,* ed. John MacArthur. (Nashville, TN: Thomas Nelson, 1997) Notes from Romans 8:15.

[28] Michael, *God's Wisdom,* 76.

[29] This list was adapted from a similar list found at http://www.blueletterbible.com.

[30] Welch, *When People Are Big and God Is Small,* 201.